W9-AKA-048

WILD RICE GOOSE
and Other Dishes of the Upper Midwest

This book was
donated by
Dennis and Barbara Manthei
2015

LA CROSSE COUNTY LIBRARY

WILD RICE GOOSE

and Other Dishes
of the Upper Midwest

John G. Motoviloff

The University of Wisconsin Press

641.691

Mo

The University of Wisconsin Press
1930 Monroe Street, 3rd Floor
Madison, Wisconsin 53711-2059
uwpress.wisc.edu

3 Henrietta Street
London WC2E 8LU, England
eurospanbookstore.com

Copyright © 2014
The Board of Regents of the University of Wisconsin System
All rights reserved. No part of this publication may be reproduced, stored in a retrieval system,
or transmitted, in any format or by any means, digital, electronic, mechanical, photocopying,
recording, or otherwise, or conveyed via the Internet or a website without written permission
of the University of Wisconsin Press, except in the case of brief quotations embedded in critical
articles and reviews.

Printed in the United States of America

Library of Congress Cataloging-in-Publication Data

Motoviloff, John, 1967–, author.
Wild rice goose and other dishes of the Upper Midwest / John G. Motoviloff.
    pages cm
    Includes index.
    ISBN 978-0-299-29904-0 (pbk. : alk. paper) — ISBN 978-0-299-29903-3 (e-book)
    1. Cooking (Game) 2. Cooking (Fish) 3. Cooking (Wild foods) 4. Cooking, Ameri-
can—Midwestern style. 5. Cooking—Middle West. I. Title.
    TX751.M68 2014
    641.59'77—dc23
    2013033114

Cover photo and design: Sara DeHaan
Book design: Caroline Beckett, Flying Fish Graphics

There's no taking of trout with dry breeches.

—*Cervantes*

CONTENTS

Preface   xi
Introduction   xiii

BIG GAME

Red-Wine Marinated Venison Steaks   6
Best Venison Burgers   7
Grilled Venison Tenderloin   8
Venison Chili   9
Venison Stew   10
Venison with Broccoli   11
Venison Meatloaf   12
Venison Pot Pie   13
Josh and Amanda Harford's Mineral Point Pasty   14
   Everything That's Old Is New Again:
    Wildfoods in the Restaurant Kitchen   15
Fruited Venison Roast   17
Bohemian Pickled Venison   18
Venison Goulash   19
Serbian Sausages with Venison   20
   What Goes into Sausage Making   21
Venison Kielbasa   22
Venison Pozole   24
Moose Stroganoff   25
Grilled Moose Chops   26
Thai Curry with Moose   27
Sweet and Sour Bear Steaks   28
Biscuits and Gravy with Ground Bear Meat   29
Bear Kotlety   30
Wild Boar Chops   31

Small Game

Best Fried Squirrel 35
Squirrel Stew 35
Squirrel with Dumplings 37
   Dressing the Part 38
Rabbit Pie 40
Rabbit Creole 41
French Rabbit with Mustard Sauce 42
Hassenpfeffer 43
Marinated Grilled Rabbit 44
Rabbit with Currants 45
Braised Snowshoe Hare 46
Denny Weiss's Roast Beaver 47

Upland Birds

Whole Roasted Pheasant 52
Pheasant Avgolemono 53
Orange Pheasant 54
Cherry Pheasant Breasts 55
Pheasant Paprikás 56
Oyster Mushrooms with Pheasant Breasts 57
   Farm-Raised Game 58
Grilled Small Gamebirds 60
Gamebirds au Vin 61
Quail à la Bud 62
Mango Wild Turkey 63

Waterfowl

Simple Roasted Duck 69
Halved Boneless Duck 70
Mushroom-Roasted Duck 71
Morel Mushroom Stroganoff 72
Currant Roasted Duck 74
Canvasback with Celery 75

Duck Gumbo   76
Duck and Barley Soup   77
Dirty Rice   78
Fancy Duck Liver Sauce   79
Wild Rice Goose   80
Wild Rice–Goose Casserole   81
    Wild Rice   82
Grilled Goose Breasts   85
Goose Tourtiere   86
Apricot Roasted Goose   87
Early Season Goose   88
Roast Goose with Sauerkraut   89
Coot in Gravy   90

FISH

Trout Cakes   98
Poached Trout with Lemon Sauce   99
Trout with Ham   100
Salmon with Chimichurri   101
Grilled Whitefish   102
    A Tough, Cold, Rewarding Job   103
Denny Weiss's Microwave Fish Fillets   106
Fried Smelt   107
Cathy Czachor's Bluegill   108
Fish Tacos   108
Fish Cakes   110
Walleye Almondine   111
Smoked Carp   112
    Making a Metal Drum Smoker   113
Pickled Fish   115
Panfried Sheepshead   116
Grilled Sturgeon   117
Turtle Soup   118
Iowa Baked Turtle   119

Crawfish Boil 120
Freshwater Fish Chowder 121
Clear Russian Fish Soup 122
Whitefish Caviar with Blini 123
  Caviar in a Half-Pound Tub? You Betcha! 124
Other Ways to Serve Whitefish Caviar 125
Baked Northern Pike 126

WILD EDIBLES

Blintzes with Fresh Berries 137
Buttermilk Pancakes with Berries 138
Berry Jam 139
Cecilia O'Brien's Mulberry Syrup 140
Black Currant Vodka 141
Classic Cobbler 142
Johnsons' Hickory Nut Pie 142
Hickory Nut Brownies 144
Basic Wild Rice 145
Wild Rice Quiche 146
Wild Mushrooms in Butter 147
  A Wild Mushroom Primer 148
Morel Mushroom Scramble 152
Puffball Fritters 153
Wild Mushroom Pierogi 154
Wild Mushrooms in Cream Sauce 156
Wild Mushroom Risotto 157
Cooking the Wild Asparagus 158
Dandelion Green Salad 159
Wild Greens Salad 160

Fish, Game, and Wildfoods Vendors 161
Index 165

PREFACE

I hope you will find this book useful, maybe even fun. In it, I've included the best of my fish and game recipes plus a few tips and tidbits here and there. Hunters, anglers, and foragers will learn new ways to cook their catch—and revisit some old favorites. I've kept the approach and recipes simple. This means beginners won't be overwhelmed by details, and seasoned kitchen hands can improvise: use shallots instead of garlic, for instance, or port instead of wine, a pinch of a favorite spice. This book is also meant for those who like wildfoods but don't get out to harvest them. Perhaps a neighbor or relative drops by with a brace of mallards, bag of morel mushrooms, panfish fillets, or a venison roast—now you'll know exactly what to do. And for those who prefer to get their wildfoods by making a trip to the store, clicking a mouse, or calling on the telephone, I've provided a list of fish, game, and wildfood vendors.

I said that I included my best fish and game recipes. This is true. But just as you need many hands to build a house, you need a bunch of outdoors friends to write a fish and game cookbook. These are the guys who go out with you to field and stream and beyond—following bird dogs through thigh-deep snow, standing in lakes that are freezing up, dragging deer out of the brambles with a tractor, hunting squirrel behind the farm, stalking spring creeks for wild trout, or hauling a canoe into the Wisconsin River. I'm lucky to count as compadres Steve Miller, Sam Diman, Dan O'Brien, Robert Pallitto, Bradley Czachor, Erik Seeman, Craig Amacker, Clarene Ditsch, and Canisius Johnson.

On the home front, my wife, Kerry Motoviloff, and daughter, Anne Motoviloff, kept things running smoothly so I could go out on wild goose chases. They were also the "tasting crew," praising me when deserved and telling me to start again when I missed the mark.

Lots of other folks helped with recipes and cooking tips. Thanks to Denny Weiss and Bill Kalishek of the Iowa DNR; Pat Rivers of the Minnesota DNR; George Wilkes of the Angry Trout Café in Grand Marais, Minnesota; Mike Valley of Valley Fish and Cheese in Prairie du Chien, Wisconsin; and the Peterson family of Hancock, Michigan. Dan O—I've got to thank you here again! To the Johnson clan of Soldiers Grove, Wisconsin, many thanks for a home away from home.

Raphael Kadushin, Matthew Crosby, Adam Mehring, Scott Lenz, and other University of Wisconsin Press staff members provided invaluable insight, guidance, and help. Thanks to the Press's reviewers for thoughtful feedback that helped make this a better book.

To Kathryn Motoviloff, Ellen Miller, and my late grandparents Michael and Anna Motoviloff, I owe a great debt of gratitude for instilling in me a love of Slavic food and culture. Thanks also to the rest of my family, who provided ample encouragement. If I've forgotten anyone, it's only because so many have helped.

INTRODUCTION

Whether pushing through swaths of prairie grass with a pair of bird dogs, jigging for whitefish on frozen Green Bay, or rumbling along sandy Northwoods roads in search of a secret berry patch, the Upper Midwest presents today's hunter-gatherer with a wide range of wildfoods and an array of landscapes in which to pursue them. This book is your guide to making the most of these treasurers. Staples for generations of Native Americans and then for the European settlers who came after them, these foods continue to provide healthy, local eating. What's more, many of these delicacies can now be purchased in person or online from a variety of vendors—from MacFarlane Pheasant Farm in southern Wisconsin to commercial fishermen on Lake Superior and a host of farmers' markets and specialty vendors in between.

Big game populations in our region remain strong. Whitetail deer are abundant. Black bear populations are holding stable. Wild pig populations have sprung up in some Midwest states. Thanks to careful Department of Natural Resources management of herds and a lottery system for licenses, Michigan hunters have the opportunity to hunt elk and Minnesota hunters have the opportunity to hunt moose.

Gamebird populations are, for the most part, alive and well. North American duck populations are well above the fifty-year average. Good goose and dove flights—and locally abundant pheasant and grouse—sweeten the wingshooter's pot. Wild turkeys have been reintroduced in much of the Upper Midwest; their numbers are strong and their range expanding northward. If woodcock, quail, and sharptail grouse numbers are spottier, this is offset by the abundance of other birds. Whether it's rich fruit-roasted duck or ruffed grouse cooked gently with forest mushrooms, Northern Tier wingshooters have plenty of birds to pursue—not to mention rabbit, snowshoe hare, and squirrel.

The culinary and sporting rewards of fish are no less thrilling. These can be familiar favorites, such as walleye taken right from the live basket to the cottage stovetop, trout from a cold spring creek poached to perfection, or fat panfish from a reedy lake fried up in a black skillet. There are also long-forgotten classics such as snapping turtle soup and upcoming foods such as whitefish caviar—highly sought after in coastal and European restaurants. Spread it on some black bread and you'll understand what all the fuss is about. We'll learn how to bread up and deep fry a batch of smelt, and to serve up rough fish like sheepshead or carp so your friends will think they're eating prime gamefish.

If it appears I have neglected wild plants, perhaps I'm saving the best for last. If you wonder whether foraging is alive and well in the twenty-first-century Northern Tier, go to a rural café or tavern on a warm May morning. The conversation will be, "Finding any little grays?" which is shorthand for "Are the first morel mushrooms up?" A few weeks later and it's off to the fencerows and ditches to hunt wild asparagus. This is followed by a profusion of wild berries: strawberries, blackcaps, gooseberries, blackberries. And then it's on to the time of nuts, wild rice, and forest mushrooms.

The point is, you won't go hungry in the Upper Midwest if you know which end of a shotgun, fishing rod, or burlap sack to pick up. You'll find old-time recipes here, like Bohemian Pickled Venison, Fruit Cobbler, and Cathy's Fried Bluegill. We'll talk to chefs from restaurants famous and humble who are featuring wildfoods on their menus. They help kick it up a notch on what Mother Nature produces—be that morel mushrooms, Great Lakes whitefish, or North Woods wild rice. To round out the view, we'll talk to trappers, hunters, sport anglers, and commercial fishermen. And, like any cookbook author, I'll add something from my own food tradition—which is decidedly Slavic. Hence, stuffed cabbage, clear fish soup, blini, and the obsession with dill, mushrooms, and sour cream.

If I've digressed, it's only because of my enthusiasm for food—food in general but particularly for what the woods and waters of the Upper Midwest have to offer. On that note, I hear that the perch are biting. I best be shoving off.

WILD RICE GOOSE

and Other Dishes
of the Upper Midwest

Big Game

As Upper Midwest lakes skim over with ice and the Vikings, Packers, and Lions vie for control of the NFC North Division, another rite of fall is in the air: deer hunting. Whether it's snowshoeing from a Northwoods deer camp, doing a drive through thick oak woods, or making long shot on a farm country whitetail, folks in these parts love to hunt deer. When gun deer season is on, everything else takes a back seat. School attendance is light, vacation days are used recklessly, chores are left undone, and bird hunting gear gets stashed away.

Now, gun deer season isn't the only kind of big game hunting in the Upper Midwest. There's bear, moose (in the far northern reaches of Minnesota), and even wild pigs in Wisconsin and other Midwest states. Bow deer season, which begins in September and goes roughly until Christmas, has its own loyal following. Ditto for the short black powder (muzzleloader) season. But if hunting is to be measured in terms of sheer economic and social impact—and by the amount of talk it receives at the local tavern—gun deer season is it.

Deer season is shrouded in tradition. It's a time for family and friends to socialize, a way to get in some visiting before winter sets in. For some hunters, it's the pursuit of a bigger buck, a higher Boone and Crockett score. But, let's face it, midwesterners are practical people. Many work in seasonal industries like forestry, building, and farming. The fifty pounds of meat they get from an average deer goes a long way toward feeding the family in winter. And if it's two or three deer, so much the better.

As with all hunting and fishing, prompt field dressing is a must for venison. The thick hide of a deer can retain heat for a day or more. The sooner the process is begun, the better the final product will be. If your deer is down and in view, wait a moment before approaching. Better still, wait five or ten minutes. Deer have a remarkable way of resurrecting themselves and sometimes a quick approach can startle the deer into calling on his adrenaline reserves—and an unpleasant chase is suddenly at hand.

Allow me to relate just such an instance from several years ago. On opening morning, a large and powerful buck walked beneath my stand. I was able to make a behind-the-shoulder shot at close range with a 303 British, and the deer went down emphatically. I followed my own rule of letting the deer lie undisturbed. As I came down the stand with my gun unloaded (for safety reasons), I heard a noise coming from the direction of the downed buck. To my horror, it was now standing up on three legs. As I hurried down the ladder, the beast marshaled whatever remaining will it had and leaped off a rock outcrop to the woods below.

I was ready now and expected to see the struggling deer on the ground. What I saw, however, was the deer somehow continuing on into the thickest possible cover. I followed. I could hear the deer moving ahead of me, but he remained hidden from view as he moved in the thicket. I followed the blood trail to a line fence that crossed a country road—and I made circles in every direction but across the road. I looked without luck for two hours, sure he had not crossed the road toward the open cover there. Long story short, the deer *had* crossed the road, and my hunting companion's neighbor called a few hours later to say that he'd found it. I tagged it, and felt very relieved.

As it was a cold day and the deer had only lain briefly, spoilage wasn't an issue. One point here is that it's good to have honest neighbors. Another is to consider even exposed escape routes when trailing a wounded deer. But the main lesson is the utter tenacity of wounded wild animals. Like crippled mallards and canvasbacks, putatively dead deer can "come back to life" in seemingly impossible and distressing ways. So wait a while—and then wait some more, before approaching a downed deer. And when you approach, have your gun ready. If all is well, tag the deer and begin gutting it.

FIELD DRESSING AND BUTCHERING

Gutting a deer is a simple task, like gutting a squirrel or rabbit but on a much larger scale. First, move the deer to a place where you can comfortably work. Some hunters carry arm-length rubber gloves to make the job cleaner. These are fine, though it can be difficult, when wearing them, to sense where your fingers are. Take extra care in knife-handling if you go this route. To begin gutting a deer, make an incision at the base of the deer's rib cage and continue the cut to the animal's anus. If you've done this before, you know what to expect. If not, be prepared for a pouring forth of blood and organs that should give you pause. This is a big animal, with a body mass and internal organs about the size of a human's. If this occasions thoughts of mortality, you're probably in the right frame of mind. Killing and gutting a big animal is a big deal.

The general idea is to let all the blood run out, so working on a slight downhill is a plus, and to carefully remove all organs (lungs, heart, liver, intestines). If the liver is intact, it can be saved for pâté or fried up as camp meat. Young deer liver is tender and mild, and liver of older deer can be soaked in buttermilk for tenderizing. The heart is also edible. Now, devote extra care to removing the intestines and do your level best not to puncture them. If you do, wipe away undigested matter as soon as possible so as not to taint the meat. Next, turn the deer cut side down so the blood can run out. Make sure to comply with all tagging and registering rules in your state.

Deer at this point can be sent to the butcher or processed yourself. In warm weather, skin and butcher the deer as soon as possible. The hide holds a great deal of heat for a long time. This is what allows them to survive our frigid winters. Now, some hunters like to "age" their deer by hanging the gutted animal in a cool, shaded place. This is fine if the weather is near the freezing point—where the deer will neither freeze nor retain heat. But this is also a game of brinksmanship because deer-season weather is rarely predictable. It can warm up, and then there is the risk of spoilage. Or it can become frigid and your deer is frozen; the deer must now be thawed to work with, and this is bad for the meat. Better to get the hide off and meat quartered and cooled (on ice or in a big refrigerator) as soon after the kill as possible. Letting meat "age" with the hide on also adds to the gamey flavor many people don't like.

With Chronic Wasting Disease (CWD) found in a small percentage of Wisconsin deer—and a smaller percentage still of Minnesota deer—many Midwest hunters are choosing to simply skin, quarter, and remove the backstrap from deer. Quartered deer can be cut into roasts or steaks, with the trimmings reserved for ground meat. I seal mine in plastic wrap or ziplocks and then wrap these packages in white butcher paper labeled with the date and cut of meat. Avoid cuts across bone and the consumption of the brain, eyes, spinal cord, lungs, spleen, tonsils, and lymph nodes. Sterilize all knives after use with a solution of ten parts water to one part bleach. As the virus for CWD lives in prions, these extra precautions minimize risk because they avoid cutting through areas—like bones and internal organs—

where lymph-dwelling prions are present. In areas of Wisconsin where CWD-infected deer have been found by the Department of Natural Resources (DNR), hunters can have their deer tested free of charge by the DNR.

The procedure for cleaning a moose is similar to that for cleaning a deer. A moose might be five or ten times the size of a deer, however. After being tagged, a moose will have to be quartered and carried out via cart or canoe or ATV (if allowed) and then cooled as soon as possible. Especially for an animal as large as moose, it is imperative that a strategy for cooling, processing, and transport be in place *before* the hunt.

Other big game animals found in the Upper Midwest, like black bears and wild pigs, are cleaned in much the same way as deer. As bear hunts take place in late summer and early fall, it's especially important to gut and skin the animal promptly. After this, the meat should be set on ice to cool. Once the meat is cooled, trim away all fat and cut it from the bone. The fat of both bears and wild pigs carries a strong and unpleasant taste. Since both wild pigs and bear can carry diseases like trichinosis, hunters should wear rubber gloves when field dressing these animals.

Big Game in the Kitchen

The sheer volume of meat from a big game animal encourages hunters to learn how to cook them well. While cleaning procedures are similar for big game animals found in the Upper Midwest, cooking approaches vary. Bear and wild pigs are heavily fatted, and should be cooked in such a way that some of the fat drains off; they should also be cooked to an internal temperature of 160 degrees. Deer and moose, on the other hand, are lean and need moisture and/or a light hand with the heat; serving these meats on the rare side will do no harm.

A number of tricks can be employed to keep venison and moose moist and palatable. When using ground venison or moose, mix in a fattier ground meat, such as pork or beef. If you are having your deer butchered, ask at the shop if they will add hamburger to your ground deer meat. Many butcher shops will do this. You can also purchase ground pork or ground beef and mix it with ground venison before cooking. A three-to-one ratio of venison or moose to fattier meat is about right. Still another option is adding suet or fatty bacon. Without the additional fat added, ground deer or moose doesn't hold together well and will make dry burgers.

For venison or moose steaks, simply marinate the meat in your favorite dressing or marinade. High-acid liquid such as wine, beer, soy sauce, or Worcestershire sauce—along with a splash of oil and pinch of herbs—will do nicely. Just watch the heat when you grill or pan-sear. Anything on the continuum of rare to medium will be juicy and flavorful; anything on the other side of this line will likely be dry and livery. Roll roasts in flour and sear on all sides for a crisp crust. Then slow-roast in a crockpot or oven with plenty of broth, wine, and vegetables. This will produce a moist, tasty roast.

You can cook wild pig in any of the ways you cook a domestic pig—roasts, chops, barbeque—and don't be afraid to experiment. Wild pig can stand up to anything you can throw at it. Fruit works well. So do sharp Asian spices. It takes to Latin flavors like cumin, chilies, and lime. East European flavors like sauerkraut, caraway, and paprika are another good complement. Always cook wild pork to an internal temperature of at least 160.

Because wild pigs and black bears consume many of the same foods—fruits, nuts, forest plants, and grubs—they are close cousins in the kitchen. Bear might be thought of as dark pork—like the dark meat on pork shoulder or close to the bone on a butt roast. Young bears are better eating than older bears; for all bear, trim away as much fat as possible because it carries strong, unpleasant flavors. Parboiling is a good option if the meat is heavily marbled. Celery, potatoes, carrots, garlic, and onions are traditionally cooked with bear roasts. Any red-wine-based marinade used for deer works well for bear loin or steak. And always cook bear to an internal temperature of at least 160 to avoid the risk of trichinosis.

Red-Wine Marinated Venison Steaks

This is a go-to recipe for marinating venison—whether burgers, steaks, or roasts. You might be tempted to use olive oil in the marinade, since it goes so well with red wine in other situations. Resist this and go with canola or vegetable oil. The stronger taste of olive oil can bring out a gamey taste in venison.

2 pounds venison steaks: medallions cut roughly into 4-ounce sections
Salt and pepper to taste

Marinade
1 cup of dry red wine
4 tablespoons canola or vegetable oil
1 teaspoon dried thyme
2 garlic cloves, crushed
¼ teaspoon salt
Pinch of black pepper

Trim venison of any skin, tendon, or fat. Salt and pepper meat on all sides. Whisk together the wine, oil, thyme, salt, and pepper. Pour over meat and marinate in stoneware or other nonreactive container for several hours. Grill or broil to medium-rare. Serve with skin-on garlic mashed potatoes.

Best Venison Burgers

Venison has too little natural fat to make good hamburgers. Adding ground pork or ground beef is a good solution. This works well for moose or any other lean ground game meat.

1 pound of ground venison
½ pound fatty ground pork or ground beef
Salt and pepper to taste

Marinade
½ cup of Worcestershire sauce
3 tablespoons peanut oil

Mix the ground meats together well and shape into 6 patties. Season with salt and pepper. Whisk together the marinade ingredients and pour over burgers. Let stand 1 hour. Cook to medium-rare over hot coals or gas grill. You can also make these in the fry pan or broiler. Serve with potato wedges, green salad, and cold beer.

Grilled Venison Tenderloin

Being essentially one long muscle, the tenderloin of any animal is both lean and tender. This prime meat is also called the backstrap. If you really want to impress your sweetheart or boss, try this recipe. Currant jam brings out bright flavor notes. Worcestershire sauce works the lower register.

1 venison tenderloin, cut into ½-inch medallions, and trimmed
    of fat and silver skin
Salt and pepper to taste
¼ cup butter

Marinade
1 garlic clove, chopped
¼ teaspoon dried thyme
½ teaspoon salt
¼ teaspoon black pepper
2 tablespoons currant jam
¼ cup Worcestershire sauce
3 tablespoons peanut oil
1 cup dry red wine

Salt and pepper venison medallions. Whisk together marinade ingredients. Put venison in nonreactive container; pour marinade over meat. Refrigerate, covered, for 1 to 4 hours. Grill or pan-sear until medium-rare. Serve with mashed potatoes, green salad, and a robust red wine such as a Cabernet.

Venison Chili

There is no better game-day food than venison chili. Now, whether to cheer for the Vikings, Lions, or Packers, that's another matter.

2 pounds ground venison (or moose)
¼ pound bacon, roughly chopped
1 green pepper, chopped
1 onion, sliced
2 garlic cloves, diced
1 tablespoon chili powder
1 teaspoon ground cumin
28-ounce can of tomatoes
2 16-ounce cans of kidney beans, with liquid
12 ounces beer
6-ounce can tomato paste
1 teaspoon salt
½ teaspoon black pepper
Dash of hot sauce, or more to taste

In a large kettle on the stovetop, brown bacon. Cook onion, garlic, and green pepper in drippings until soft; add venison and cook until done. Add chili powder, cumin, tomatoes, beans, beer, and tomato paste. Cook for 1 hour; season with salt, pepper, and hot sauce. Let simmer until guests arrive. Serve over rice or pasta noodles. Sour cream, grated cheese, and minced onions are good go-withs.

Venison Stew

Venison stew conjures up images of an old black kettle bubbling away on the back burner. And it somehow warms you to the bone—whether you've been out hunting, snow-shoeing, ice fishing, splitting wood, or just grocery shopping on a cold day. Another virtue is that venison stew can be taken in any number of directions depending on the ingredients on hand and the inclinations of the cook. Rutabagas, turnips, parsnips, cabbage, and mushrooms are all at home here. Substitute dark beer for wine and it comes close to Irish stew. Add oregano and up the garlic and you have something like a Greek *stifado*. Paprika, caraway seeds, and sour cream take the flavors toward Eastern Europe. Whatever ethnic direction you choose, however, you'll also need a dose of patience. Stew must be cooked low and slow.

> 2 pounds venison, cut into chunks
> Flour seasoned with salt and pepper
> ¼ cup butter
> 1 onion, sliced
> 1 garlic clove, minced
> 1 cup dry red wine
> 1 cup beef broth
> ¼ teaspoon dried thyme
> 1 bay leaf
> 2 carrots, peeled and chopped
> 4 potatoes, peeled and chopped
> Salt and pepper to taste

Heat butter in the bottom of a large kettle. Brown venison along with the onion and garlic. Add wine, broth, thyme, bay leaf, carrots, and potatoes. Simmer 1½ hours or until meat is tender. Add salt and pepper to taste. Serve in bowls, accompanied by French bread and plenty of red wine.

Venison with Broccoli

This is a wild-game take on Chinese beef with broccoli. Mushrooms are optional, but in my opinion they add nice brown flavor.

2 pounds venison, cut into 1-inch by 2-inch slices, fat removed
1 head of broccoli, cut into florets
1 onion, sliced
2 garlic cloves, peeled
½ cup button or shitake mushrooms, chopped (optional)
¼ cup vegetable or peanut oil
2 tablespoons cornstarch

Marinade
¾ cup soy sauce
¼ cup red wine or sherry
2 garlic cloves, crushed
1 teaspoon grated ginger root, or ¼ teaspoon powdered ginger
¼ teaspoon ground black pepper
Dash of chili oil or 2 dried chili peppers
¼ cup vegetable or peanut oil

Combine marinade ingredients and whisk together. Put venison in a nonreactive container and pour marinade over it. Marinate, covered, in the refrigerator for 1 to 4 hours. Drain marinade and reserve. Heat oil in wok or large skillet; brown venison quickly and remove with slotted spoon. (It should still be rare when you remove it.) Set venison aside. In the same wok or skillet, add the garlic, onion, broccoli, and optional mushrooms. Cook until broccoli is just shy of done—it will be bright green—and add reserved marinade. Cook marinade for 5 minutes, stir in cornstarch. (Add water if you want more sauce.) Replace the venison pieces and cook just until done. Serve over white rice or thin noodles.

VENISON MEATLOAF

You can put just about anything in a meatloaf. That's both its strength and the reason it can be god-awful. Good meatloaves tend toward a unified taste—Mexican, Italian, down-home, or what have you. Things go awry when the taste families get mixed together. Below is a recipe for a basic meatloaf. Possible add-ins are leftover tortillas, chilies, corn and black beans; Italian seasoning and parmesan cheese; or cheddar cheese, barbeque sauce, and bacon.

    1 pound ground venison
    ½ pound ground beef or pork
    2 tablespoons canola oil
    1 onion, sliced
    1 garlic clove, minced
    1 egg, beaten
    ½ cup bread crumbs
    Dash of Worcestershire sauce
    Dash of hot sauce, or more to taste
    ½ teaspoon green herbs such as thyme, rosemary, or oregano

Preheat oven to 350 degrees. Grease a baking pan with butter or oil. Mix together the two meats. Sauté the onion and garlic. When cooled, add these to the meat, along with the egg, bread crumbs, Worcestershire sauce, hot sauce, and green herbs. Mix until ingredients are uniform throughout. Shape into loaf and place into a greased baking pan. Bake 45 minutes. Serve with mashed potatoes and steamed green beans.

Venison Pot Pie

There's something deeply comforting in sitting down to a steaming pot pie, especially if you've harvested the meat that goes into it.

1 pound of venison or moose, ground or chopped fine
1 onion, chopped
1 large potato, cubed
1 carrot, cut into large dice
1 small rutabaga, peeled and cubed, or 1 cup of cabbage, chopped
4 tablespoons butter
½ cup of red wine or dark beer
Salt and pepper to taste
Dried thyme to taste
2 9-inch pie crusts (store-bought or home-made)
3 tablespoons sour cream, or more to taste

Preheat oven to 350 degrees. Melt butter in the bottom of a large skillet. Sauté onion and add venison and cook until just done; add potato, carrot, and rutabaga or cabbage. Cook until soft, adding water if necessary. Add wine or beer and seasonings. Grease a 9-inch baking dish and line with one pie crust. Place meat filling on crust and place sour cream on top of meat. Cover with top crust, crimp edges, and cut vents in pie. Bake for ½ hour or until golden-brown. Serve with applesauce or green salad.

Josh and Amanda Harford's Mineral Point Pasty

As I was finishing up this book, I got a call from our friends the Harfords of Cottage Grove, Wisconsin, asking if my daughter would like to stay at their house for a dinner of venison pasties. I knew her food tastes enough to answer an emphatic Yes. As I continued with the manuscript, however, the words "venison pasty" kept creeping into my mind. I realized, to my horror, I had no recipe for this go-to Upper Midwest food in the book! Josh and Amanda Harford were kind enough to supply this recipe. They both grew up on farms near Mineral Point, where pasties have been a staple since Cornish miners settled the area in the 1820s. So you know this recipe is tried and true. Amanda notes that her grandmother used to use equal parts lard and butter in her crusts. Make your own or use store bought, according to your preference.

> 1 pound ground venison
> ¼ pound ground pork or hamburger
> 1 onion, chopped
> 2 potatoes, peeled and diced
> 1 cup turnip, peeled and diced (optional)
> Salt and pepper to taste
> 2 9-inch pie crusts (store-bought or home-made)
> 4 tablespoons butter

Preheat oven to 350 degrees. Mix the ground meats together well and brown in a large skillet; set meat aside in bowl. In drippings that are produced, brown the vegetables until just tender; add water if additional moisture is needed. Combine meat and vegetables. Salt and pepper to taste. Cut both pie crusts in half, so you have four pieces. Place two half-circles of crust on a baking sheet. Fill with meat and vegetable mixture, top with remaining crusts, crimp edges, and cut slits in the top-middle of each pasty. You should have two crescent-shaped pies. Place butter in the slits and bake for 40 or 45 minutes.

Everything That's Old Is New Again:
Wildfoods in the Restaurant Kitchen

If you look at menus from restaurants in nineteenth-century America, you'll see a lot of wild fish and game. From cottontail rabbit to canvasback duck and from whitetail deer to Lake Michigan whitefish, eateries dished out the bounty that Mother Nature provided. This made sense when there were few people and abundant wildlife. But as the nation matured, human populations began to grow and game numbers began to dwindle. Market hunting (the source of restaurant game) was outlawed in the early twentieth century, and Great Lakes fisheries were showing signs of decline. Also, after World War II, consumer tastes were shifting to newer foods and food venues, such as supper clubs, fast food, and ethnic restaurants. Processed and prepared foods also emerged. But something began to shift toward the end of the twentieth century. Call it a return to the roots, a yearning for nostalgia, a trend toward low-fat eating, or just a swing of the pendulum. Game and wild-caught fish began to reappear on restaurant menus.

Today's wildfoods differ from early commercial fish and game in one important way: they are responsibly harvested. Game farms allow for the rearing of these delicacy meats without affecting wildlife populations, and commercial fishing is tightly controlled by state and federal laws. Still, the craving for native Upper Midwest foods persists. The Angry Trout Café in Grand Marais, Minnesota, serves up four local, wild-harvested foods: Lake Superior fish, Canadian wild blueberries, and Minnesota wild rice and maple syrup. Owner Georges Wilkes says, "We started to focus on local and sustainable foods in the early 1990s. There's no comparison in quality. Mother Nature does a really good job of providing really good food."

While Wilkes focuses on local fish and wild plants, Michigan restaurant owner "Dixie" Dave Minar has been dubbed the Guru of Game. Minar has appeared extensively on cable TV as a game cook, and does banquets for conservation groups such as Ducks Unlimited and Pheasants Forever. The restaurant he operates, Oscar and Joey's Roadhouse, has a separate game menu featuring elk, game sausage, venison, and buffalo. An avid hunter who grew up eating all sorts of game, Minar has a simple philosophy on game cooking: "It's the most wonderful food on the face of the earth. Don't overcook it."

Wilkes's and Minar's establishments are among a growing number in the Upper Midwest that serve wildfoods. Venison, buffalo, elk, wild boar, pheasant, quail, rabbit, Great Lakes fish and caviar, wild rice, wild mushrooms, wild greens, and wild berries are some common wildfood options. Looking to add some wild to your dining? Here are a few more—Heartland and the Corner Table in the Twin Cities; Wild Rice in Bayfield and L'Etoile in Madison, Wisconsin; Harbor Haus in Copper Harbor, Ernie and Joey's Roadhouse in Birch Run, and Beaver Creek Lodge, Deadwood Bar and Grill, the Moose Preserve, and Camp Ticonderoga in the Greater Detroit area. Loon River Café in Sterling Heights, Michigan, and Harvest Restaurant in Madison, Wisconsin, feature a "game dinner night" each fall.

Fruited Venison Roast

Fruit often shows up in gamebird recipes, but it also works well with venison. Moose can be substituted for venison here.

> 4- or 5-pound venison roast trimmed of fat
> 3 garlic cloves, sliced
> Flour seasoned with salt and pepper
> 1 teaspoon dried green herbs such as thyme, marjoram, rosemary,
>   and/or oregano
> ¼ cup bacon drippings or butter
> 1 package of mixed dried fruit—prunes, apricots, cranberries, etc.
> 1 cup beef broth
> 2 more tablespoons broth for optional gravy

Preheat oven to 300 degrees. Pierce roast in 12 or more places and insert garlic slivers; dredge roast in flour. Season with green herbs. Melt drippings or butter in large skillet and brown roast on all sides. Place browned roast in covered roasting pan; add dried fruit and beef broth. Bake until tender—2 to 2½ hours. Serve with mashed potatoes and cranberry sauce. To serve roaster juices as gravy, remove roast and heat pan—on stovetop over medium heat—stirring in 2 tablespoons flour and cooking until there are no lumps.

Bohemian Pickled Venison

This is a time-consuming, several-days-in-the-making dish, but well worth it. Like sauerbraten, it calls for a long soak in a vinegar bath, and then slow cooking that makes it fork-tender. Students of history may be interested in knowing that Bohemians were the first Slavic immigrants to come to the Upper Midwest, having arrived as early as the mid-nineteenth century. Northern Michigan, northeastern and southwestern Wisconsin, north-eastern Iowa, and southern Minnesota all have communities settled by Bohemians.

4- or 5-pound venison roast, trimmed of fat
4 tablespoons butter
1 cup sour cream
1 tablespoon flour
1 tablespoon brown sugar

Marinade
2 cups of vinegar
12 ounces beer
1 onion, sliced
½ teaspoon salt
10 black peppercorns
10 allspice berries
4 whole cloves
1 bay leaf
2 inch-long pieces of lemon peel, chopped

Place venison roast in a large, nonreactive vessel. Whisk together marinade ingredients, then cover roast with marinade. Cover and let stand in the refrigerator for two days. Remove roast from marinade and pat dry; reserve marinade. Melt butter in a large kettle and brown roast well on all sides. Add reserved marinade and cook on lowest possible heat until meat starts to shred. Remove meat to heated platter. At this point, remove 1 cup of marinade and add to it to the sour cream, flour, and brown sugar. Add sour-cream mixture to cooking liquid and heat until sauce thickens. Serve cream gravy on the side of meat with fresh rye bread and dumplings, egg noodles, or mashed potatoes.

Venison Goulash

Hungarians in the Upper Midwest have tended to settle near cities such as Detroit, Milwaukee, and St. Paul to work in large industries. Enthusiasm for the hunt and a love of good food runs strong in Hungarian culture, however. Please note that authentic Hungarian goulash is not a slapdash mixture of ground beef and elbow noodles, but a brick-red stew that is given its unique color and flavor from paprika. Use good paprika, like Szeged or Budapest's Best, available in most grocery stores, sweet or spicy according to your preference. Store paprika in the refrigerator, as it's made from dried peppers and their oil goes rank when left at room temperature.

> **3 tablespoons canola or sunflower oil**
> **1 large onion, sliced**
> **1½ pounds venison cut into 1-inch dice**
> **2 tablespoons paprika**
> **½ teaspoon marjoram**
> **½ teaspoon caraway seeds**
> **1 cup water, or more as needed**
> **1 carrot, peeled and chopped**
> **1 tomato, chopped**
> **1 large potato, peeled and chopped**
> **Salt and pepper to taste**
> **½ cup sour cream (optional)**

Heat oil in large skillet or Dutch oven and add onions; cook on low until they are soft. Do not burn. Add meat and cook with onions for 10 minutes; add paprika, marjoram, and caraway seeds. Stir to make sure meat is coated in spices. Add water and remaining ingredients, except salt and pepper. Cook for 1½ hours or until meat is tender. Add salt and pepper to taste. Pass sour cream, at table, if desired. Serve with rye bread and wide egg noodles or mashed potatoes. A lager along the lines of Pilsner Urquell, or a hearty red wine, will round out the meal.

SERBIAN SAUSAGES WITH VENISON

Small but vibrant Serbian communities can be found throughout the Upper Midwest, including enclaves in Milwaukee, Detroit, and the Twin Cities. Serbs also settled in the Iron Range country of Michigan, Wisconsin, and Minnesota to work in the mining and lumber industries. As with other ethnic groups, Serbians brought old-country delicacies to the New World. Plum brandy (*slivovitz*), thin pancakes (*palacsinta*), and these tasty, hand-rolled sausages (*cevapcici*) are a few examples. *Cevapcici* are typically made with domestic meats such as beef and pork, but venison mixed with these is equally good. They can be an appetizer or, served with a starch like rice, a main course. A cucumber-yogurt salad, similar to *tzatziki*, is the traditional accompaniment.

> 2 pounds ground venison
> 1 pound ground beef, pork, or a mixture of the two
> 1 onion, minced
> 2 garlic cloves, minced
> 2 tablespoons hot paprika
> 1 teaspoon salt
> ½ teaspoon black pepper
> 2 tablespoons olive oil, or more as needed

In a large bowl, combine the different meats and mix well. Add onion, garlic, paprika, salt, and pepper to the meat; mix these ingredients evenly throughout. Form into sausages about the size of a cigar and coat with olive oil. Refrigerate 1 hour and cook over charcoal grill or under the broiler. This goes well with a cucumber-yogurt salad and some crusty bread.

What Goes into Sausage Making

When I got a book on home sausage making for Christmas some years ago, I was intrigued. You mean kielbasa, chorizo, andouille, Italian—all that great stuff in the butcher case—can be made at home? But I couldn't quite delve in. I had questions: Where do you get casings? How do you get the ground meat into those tiny things? And am I going to get food poisoning? There was an order-of-magnitude leap from trying a new recipe to learning a new branch of cooking. I hemmed and hawed. I ate some sausage. I read the cookbook some more. On a trip to Jim's Meats in on the north side of Madison for bratwurst, I found they carried sausage casings, or cleaned pig's intestine. As Easter was approaching and I planned to break my Lenten fast with kielbasa—the real, juicy, garlicky stuff of my New Jersey youth—I decided to take the plunge. I found Smoked Kielbasa on page 141 of *Home Sausage Making* by Susan Mahnke Peery and Charles G. Reavis. Nothing in the ingredients looked all that intimidating. And I had lots of pork roasts. I didn't have beef on hand, but why not substitute venison from the deer I shot the previous fall? I was finally ready to give it a try.

Cubing, grinding, and seasoning were all pretty basic. I felt comfortable enough with my food instincts to tamper a bit. Why not add caraway seeds and up the garlic? But the big question persisted: How do you get all that ground meat into those tiny little casings? Now, a normal person would probably have gone down to the farm and home store and bought sausage-stuffing equipment. In fact, that's exactly what my wife suggested as I stood over the sink for hours, threading the sausage casing onto the tube of a turkey baster and pushing the meat into the casing with a homemade pestle. And that's still what she says, as I use my improvised sausage-making tools. But it's been ten years now, and I've somehow made it work—a little faster each year and still no trip to the farm and home store. I would direct readers to a farm-and-home or cooking store to buy commercial equipment. But I must say, there's a certain DIY satisfaction in doing things the Robinson Crusoe way.

How's the sausage? It's great! Better than anything I buy in the store. I'm the boss. I have complete control over the ingredients. The pork comes from a friend's farm in southwest Wisconsin. The venison is from deer I shoot. The spices and herbs are fresh. Since I like a kick, I add cayenne. If I think it should go in, it goes in. If I don't think it should go in, it doesn't. I smoke the sausage at 200 degrees for 2 hours—until the internal temperature is 160—and plunge it into ice water to help set. (All home sausage makers need a reliable meat thermometer; they should always cook to proper internal temperature.) Before the midnight Easter Liturgy, I set the kielbasa on a cloth in my Easter basket, rope it around a rich bread called *kulich* and a sweet cheese called *syrniya pascha*, have it blessed, and enjoy it with family and friends.

I still don't know what goes into politics, but I have a pretty good idea what goes into my sausage.

VENISON KIELBASA

Once you get beyond the fact that stuffing meat into a tiny tube is just plain tedious, even with the help of specialized equipment, you realize that homemade sausage has a lot going for it. Don't like marjoram? Then leave it out. Like a lot of garlic? Then add a few more cloves. And there's no doubt about the ingredients when you make the sausage your-self—you have complete control. I make venison kielbasa for Easter to go along with ham, horseradish, boiled eggs, pickles, and potato salad. It's also delicious served as a main dish, with a side of sauerkraut and applesauce. It's terrific sautéed with peppers and onions, slathered with mustard, and served on a crusty roll. And it's equally at home on the breakfast table with fried eggs, rye toast, and strong coffee. While the spices in this recipe can be modified, the pork must have some fat to it. Otherwise, the sausage will be too dry. Bear in mind that this sausage must "cure" for 24 hours in the refrigerator before it's cooked, so plan accordingly. Casing is available at some butcher shops and online at sausagemaker.com.

> 4 feet medium hog casing (ask butcher for enough casing
>   for 5 pounds of sausage)
> 3 pounds pork shoulder or pork butt with fat, cut into 1-inch cubes
> 2 pounds venison, trimmed of fat and silver skin,
>   and cut into 1-inch cubes
> Curing salt (follow directions on package for 5 pounds of meat)
> 1 tablespoon hot paprika
> 1 tablespoon brown sugar
> 1 teaspoon black pepper
> ½ teaspoon caraway seeds (optional)
> 3 garlic cloves, diced
> ½ teaspoon marjoram
> ½ teaspoon coriander

Freeze meat cubes for ½ hour, then grind coarse with food processor or meat grinder. Mix meat together; add spices. Stuff mixture into sausage casing using a funnel or your fingers. Do not overstuff. Prick a few small holes into each length of sausage to help keep casing from breaking. Tie off into convenient lengths (12 to 16 inches works well) by knotting casing. Refrigerate for 24 hours. Smoke sausage for 2 hours, at about 200 degrees. Check to make sure sausage reaches 160 degrees internal temperature. Plunge smoked sausage into pan of ice water for ½ hour. This helps it set. Enjoy cold, as you would summer sausage, or browned in a skillet.

Venison Pozole

This classic Mexican soup, often served on Christmas Eve, works well with venison.

2 pounds venison cut into chunks
1 onion, roughly chopped
4 garlic cloves, chopped
2 tablespoons canola oil
1 teaspoon cumin
½ teaspoon dried oregano (preferably Mexican)
2 14½-ounce cans of enchilada sauce (hot or mild, depending
    on preference)
2 16-ounce cans hominy, drained
1 cup of chicken broth
Salt to taste

Heat oil in the bottom of a large kettle. Brown venison along with the onion and garlic. Add cumin, oregano, enchilada sauce, hominy, and chicken broth and simmer for 2 hours or until meat is tender. Check for salt (many enchilada sauces are high in salt, so you may not need much). Serve with cornbread or corn tortillas and sour cream.

Moose Stroganoff

This recipe and the two recipes following it are courtesy of Pat Rivers, a large-lake fisheries biologist with the Minnesota DNR. After applying to the Minnesota DNR's lottery for moose hunting, Pat was lucky enough to receive a permit. He shot a big bull moose in Minnesota's Boundary Waters that yielded some four hundred pounds of meat. So Pat has had plenty of experience cooking moose. According to him, "Moose has a nice mild flavor, but it can be lean and tough, especially older animals." Marinating or slow cooking are good ways to tenderize it.

> 1 pound moose steak cut into 1-inch pieces
> Salt and pepper to taste
> ¼ cup butter, or more as needed
> 1 cup fresh mushrooms, chopped
> 1 onion, chopped
> 1 garlic clove, minced
> 1 cup sour cream
>
> *Marinade*
> 1 cup sherry, port, or Marsala wine
> 1 teaspoon sugar
> ¼ cup vegetable oil
> ½ teaspoon black pepper
> 1 teaspoon salt

Salt and pepper moose; whisk together marinade ingredients. Let meat marinate, refrigerated and in nonreactive container, for 4 hours or overnight. Drain meat well and reserve marinade. In a large wok or skillet, melt butter. Quickly sauté moose. Do not overcook. Remove with a slotted spoon. Add additional butter or cooking oil if necessary. Cook mushrooms, onion, and garlic until soft. Add reserved marinade and cook on high for 5 minutes. Replace meat; cook until just done. Turn off heat. When sauce stops bubbling, stir in sour cream. Serve immediately over wide egg noodles. A golden lager or robust red wine will do the moose proud.

Grilled Moose Chops

The same basic ingredients—onions, mushrooms, and game meat—are used here as for Moose Stroganoff. While Stroganoff is warm and comforting, the grilling treatment here gets the caveman endorphins flowing. What's a surprise to many is that moose is actually milder than venison. The challenge is keeping it moist—hence the Italian salad dressing. This is a good deer camp meal and can be made with venison.

> 2 pounds moose chops
> 1 bottle good-quality Italian salad dressing—such as
>   Ken's Steakhouse brand
> 1 onion, chopped
> 1 cup mushrooms, sliced
> 2 tablespoons oil or butter

Place chops in nonreactive container, such as stainless steel, enameled pot, or stoneware. Cover with the Italian dressing as a marinade and allow to marinate for at least 4 hours. Drain chops and discard marinade. Preheat gas grill to 350 degrees or have charcoal briquettes ashed-over and gray. Heat a skillet on the stovetop; sauté onions and mushrooms and keep them warm. Cook chops 2½ minutes per side, or until medium-rare. Serve with sautéed onions and mushrooms, mashed potatoes, and a green salad.

Thai Curry with Moose

While curry is a very different flavor treatment than onions and mushrooms, it's another good way to get the meat tender. Don't hesitate to substitute venison for moose. And who doesn't like the burn of a good curry?

13½-ounce can of coconut milk
1 or 2 tablespoons red Thai curry paste, such as
    Thai Kitchen or Roland
2 tablespoons brown sugar
2 tablespoons soy sauce
1 cup fresh basil, roughly chopped
1 pound moose meat cut into chunks
2 cups of diced onion and green pepper
1 cup peapods (optional)

In a large saucepan, combine coconut milk, curry paste, brown sugar, soy sauce, and basil. Mix well and cook for 5 minutes. Add moose, onions, and peppers. Cook until moose is tender—usually about 1 hour. Cooking time will vary depending on the age of the moose. Try a small piece to see if it's done to your liking. Add optional peapods and cook for 5 minutes more, until they are bright green. Serve over cooked white rice.

SWEET AND SOUR BEAR STEAKS

Young bear is tender and mild. Older animals are stronger in flavor, but still good eating with the help of the right ingredients, as in this sweet and sour treatment. This recipe is also good with wild pig.

> 4 pounds bear steaks, or a roast cut into chunks, trimmed of fat
> Salt, pepper, and paprika to taste
> Flour for dredging
> 4 tablespoons bacon drippings or salad oil
> 1 onion, sliced
> 2 garlic cloves, chopped
> 4 dried chili peppers
> 12 ounces beer
> 12 ounces apple juice or cider
> ¼ cup cider vinegar
> 1 cup chicken broth
> 2 tablespoons brown sugar
> 1 cup sour cream and 2 tablespoons flour (optional)

Season bear meat and then dredge in flour. Heat a large kettle or Dutch oven on the stovetop; melt bacon drippings. Brown bear well on all sides. Add onion and garlic; cook until tender. Add chili peppers, beer, apple juice, vinegar, and sugar. Cook until bear is tender—about 2 hours. If you want a thicker stew, remove ½-cup of cooking liquid; mix it into a paste with flour and sour cream. Return this paste to the stew and stir until dissolved and stew has returned to the boil; serve immediately. Serve with crusty bread, applesauce, and cold beer.

BISCUITS AND GRAVY WITH GROUND BEAR MEAT

Denny Weiss, of Bellevue, Iowa, hunts bear in Ontario and Minnesota. He was kind enough to share this recipe with me. As bear hunts often take place in early fall or late summer, Denny quickly guts and skins the bear, then places the quartered meat on ice in a cooler. Once it's cooled, he trims away the fat and debones the meat.

1 pound ground bear meat
½ pound ground pork
1 teaspoon sausage seasoning
1 onion, peeled and chopped
2 tablespoons flour
2 cup milk, heated

Mix together bear meat and pork; add seasoning. If you can't find sausage seasoning, add salt, black pepper, and green herbs of your choice (such as thyme, marjoram, or rosemary). Brown meat in a heavy skillet; add onions and cook until soft. Dust with flour and mix well. Add milk and cook on low flame for 5 minutes. Serve over hot biscuits.

BEAR KOTLETY

These meat patties, often made with pork or veal, are a mainstay in Slavic countries. It's a nice change from regular hamburgers and suited to the well-fatted meat of bear. The ingredients are very basic; chances are you have them on hand. You can make *kotlety* with venison or moose, but add ground pork to help them stay moist—½ pound for every pound of moose or venison.

> 1½ pounds ground bear meat, or 1 pound ground venison/moose
>   and ½ pound ground pork
> 1 onion, minced
> 1 garlic clove, minced
> 1 cup of bread crumbs, or 3 slices of stale white bread,
>   crust removed, and chopped
> 1 egg, beaten
> Salt and pepper to taste
> 1 tablespoon fresh or dried dill (optional)
> 2 tablespoons oil, or more as needed

Freeze ground meat for 10 minutes; remove from freezer. Combine cold meat, onion, garlic, bread crumbs, and egg; mix well. Season as desired with salt, pepper, and optional dill. Form into patties. Roll again in bread crumbs if you want patties extra crispy. Heat oil in skillet. Fry patties until brown on both sides. Bear, like pork, should be cooked until well done, or 160 degrees at the center. Serve with cranberry sauce and mashed potatoes.

WILD BOAR CHOPS

The wild pigs now living in southwest Wisconsin are likely the offspring of released game-farm pigs. Michigan, Iowa, and Minnesota also have wild pig populations. While Wisconsin encourages hunters to shoot wild pigs—which are nonnative and destructive to crops and wildlife habitat—other states have not yet established a hunting season for them. Check your state's regulations. You can also order wild pig/boar from a number of vendors including MacFarlane Pheasant Farm. Wild pigs have lean meat and good flavor.

2 pounds chops or steaks from wild pigs, trimmed of all fat
Salt and pepper to taste
½ cup olive oil
1 cup white wine
½ teaspoon dried thyme
2 garlic cloves, chopped
1 tablespoon paprika

Generously salt and pepper meat. Combine the remaining five ingredients and whisk together. Place chops in stoneware or other nonreactive bowl, cover with marinade, and allow to stand for 2 hours. Grill over medium heat until internal temperature reaches 160 degrees. Serve with herb-roasted potatoes and green salad.

SMALL GAME

Somewhere along the line, things have gotten too fast and too big. Hunting is too often about the biggest buck or turkey with the longest beard, and fishing is an exercise in expensive electronics and gear. Instead of becoming a means to an end, gear and technique seem more like ends in themselves. The easiest way to turn your back on this is to go into the squirrel woods or rabbit patch with a few shells in your pocket. Whether you're watching the limbs of an old oak tree or nudging a brush pile with your boot and scanning for fleeting shapes, you'll be immersed in what you're doing. Lost in what you're doing. Enjoying what the Spanish essayist Ortega y Gasset calls "a vacation from the human condition."

As I'm writing these words, I realize squirrel season is just a few days off, and I'll soon be leaning against the fencerow-corner of my land, waiting, looking, listening. And as the light dims to evening, the first silhouette of a gray squirrel will appear, twitching its bushy tail, on a hickory limb. Or perhaps I'll hear nuts dropping onto the leaves below. Or make out that rustling sound—louder than seems possible—of a squirrel shuffling about. Maybe it's childish for a man in his mid-forties to become so animated over a small animal. But if that's the case, so be it. There are greater vices.

There is of course the winter version of this woodland idyll, where the hunter picks along a thicket or blackberry or multiflora rose, moving softly, perhaps on snowshoes, wearing just a wool shirt and brush pants. Here, the telltale triangle tracks of rabbits! There, a trail of round droppings!

A loose knot of crows calls from the birch tree in the distance. There's blue sky overhead and white snow underfoot. You see a movement in the bushes—a brown form darting away—and you quickly pivot.

I hope the point is clear: there's much sport in small game hunting. If you remain unconvinced, get out and try it. At the very least, you'll get exercise and fresh air. But if the conditions are right—seasonable weather, without much wind—you have a good chance at success. All this, though, and I still haven't mentioned eating. Forget—or embrace—the red-neck image that goes along with small game hunting. Forget that rabbits are supposed to be cute and cuddly. And think for a moment about animals that eat nuts and wild fruit; or buds, tender greens, and waste grain. Think about lean, wild meat stewed with mushrooms. Now you see a entirely different reason for going out.

Like many great foods, small game can be dressed up or down, elegant or simple, ethnic or down home. Stewed with mushrooms, roasted with mustard and herbs, marinated for Hassenpfeffer, rabbit is a versatile and overlooked delicacy. If you prefer comfort food, there are few meals more soul-nourishing than a flaky-crusted rabbit pie. Domestic rabbit is a good substitute for wild rabbit and is available in specialty stores, farmers' markets, and online at MacFarlane Pheasant Farm. Rabbit, whether wild or domestic, is mild in flavor and delicious. Squirrel is smaller in size, but equally delicious. The meat is rosy, with a distinctive nutty flavor. Both squirrel and rabbit benefit from a brief parboiling; this helps tenderize the meat. Squirrel can be substituted for rabbit and vice versa. A rabbit, with side dishes, serves two or three. One squirrel, with sides, serves one or two.

Both rabbits and squirrels are easy to clean, and should be taken care of in the field, immediately after being shot. Make an incision close to the hind legs and work one leg—foot and all—through the incision. For squirrels, simply stand on the tail, grab hold of the skin and pull toward the head. Cut off feet at first joint. Remove entrails. The procedure is almost identical for a rabbit, but the tail is too small to stand on. Once the hind leg is slipped through the incision, simply work the skin toward the head, pulling with moderate pressure, and it should come off in one piece. Remove entrails. For both rabbit and squirrel, allow animal to cool after removing entrails. Blot the inside with leaves, grass, or paper towel.

I keep a burlap bag in my vest pocket and put the cooled animals in it. Any breathable fabric—or mesh citrus bag—will work for this purpose. In cold weather, a ziplock bag is OK, but in warm weather it traps the heat. Prior to cooking rabbits or squirrels, rinse off any fur or debris; soak them in cold salted water to help clot shot-damaged portions. Whether at home or in the field, the animals can be cut into serving pieces—two hind legs, two front legs, and the back (cut in half on larger animals). For animals that will be frozen, seal in plastic wrap (or a ziplock with excess air forced out of it) and wrap in butcher paper.

Rabbit and squirrel are the most commonly hunted small game animals, but not the only ones. Snowshoe hare can be found in the Northwoods. While they are rarely targeted specifically, snowshoe hare are sometimes taken as a part of a "mixed bag" on bird hunts. They can be tougher and stronger-tasting than cottontail rabbit, but are worth eating—especially since they are about twice the size of an average cottontail. Soak hares in buttermilk or vinegar water prior to cooking. Parboiling also helps with tenderizing.

In wooded farm country—such as Iowa, southern Wisconsin, and southern Michigan—some hunters still enjoy taking part in the old-fashioned sport of raccoon hunting with hounds. Some hunters hunt for the fur, but young raccoons make for good eating. They are cleaned in much the same way as a rabbit or squirrel. Make sure to remove the glands located beneath the front arms of the carcass, and trim away the fat. Any recipe for squirrel or rabbit will also work for raccoon. Also, I've included a beaver recipe for trappers who might buy this book. As with raccoons, young beavers make for better eating; fat and scent glands need to be removed.

BEST FRIED SQUIRREL

Squirrel is probably the most underappreciated game meat. Squirrel hunters and their friends, however, know it's tender and full of flavor. In this recipe, it resembles fried chicken—but tastes better.

> 2 squirrels, cleaned and cut into serving pieces
> Flour seasoned with salt, pepper, and ¼ teaspoon poultry seasoning
> 4 tablespoons vegetable oil; or 2 tablespoons oil and 2 tablespoons butter

Parboil squirrel pieces for 5 minutes and allow to cool; dredge in seasoned flour. Heat a large skillet to medium-hot and add the oil or oil-butter mixture. Gently brown squirrel well on all sides. Add additional butter or oil if needed. When tender—between 30 and 45 minutes depending on the size of the squirrels—remove from skillet. Serve with applesauce, cornbread, and cooked turnip or mustard greens.

SQUIRREL STEW

A good hearty game stew, served piping hot on a cold night, ranks right up there with grilled venison or roast mallard. This recipe is probably somewhere between a Brunswick Stew and Burgoo. Being a Northerner, I can't pin down, exactly, what distinguishes one from the other, so I will take the safe route and simply call this Squirrel Stew. The combination of meats adds to the rich flavor, as do the tomatoes, corn, Worcestershire sauce, and hot sauce.

> 2 squirrels, cleaned and cut into serving pieces
> 2 pounds cut-up chicken parts (thighs, breasts, drumsticks);
>   or 1 pheasant or grouse cut into serving pieces
> 1 pound venison, cut into chunks

1 gallon water

2 onions, sliced

2 garlic cloves, minced

1 green pepper, chopped

4 tablespoons bacon drippings or peanut oil

4 tablespoons flour

28-ounce can of tomatoes

½ pound good-quality smoked ham, diced

3 red potatoes with skin on, cubed

16-ounce can of corn

½ teaspoon dried thyme

2 tablespoons Worcestershire sauce

Dash of hot sauce, or more to taste

Salt and pepper to taste

1 cup of any of the following—green or wax beans, chopped cabbage,
    chopped carrots (optional)

In a large kettle or cauldron, bring water to boiling. Add squirrel, choice of birds, and venison. Cook on low flame until all is tender. Debone the squirrel and bird; shred the venison. Strain and reserve the cooking liquid. In a separate pot large enough to hold all the ingredients, heat the oil or drippings and cook the onion, garlic, and green pepper until tender. Add flour and stir until lightly browned. Now add reserved cooking liquid, stirring so the flour mixes in with it. Replace deboned meats. Add the tomatoes, ham, potatoes, corn, thyme, and Worcestershire sauce. If using any of the optional vegetables, add at this point. After stew simmers for a while, add hot sauce, salt, and pepper to taste. Serve in bowls with cornbread on the side.

SQUIRREL WITH DUMPLINGS

Frugal and full of flavor, this dish is much like chicken and dumplings, but with the richer taste of squirrel. The cornmeal dumpling recipe here is very close to the one found in *Joy of Cooking*. The herbs are my addition. You can substitute your own dumpling recipe for this one if you have a favorite.

2 quarts chicken broth
2 squirrels, cleaned and cut into serving pieces
1 onion, sliced
2 celery stalks, diced
2 carrots, sliced or chunked
1 bay leaf
½ teaspoon thyme or poultry seasoning
1 teaspoon salt, or to taste
½ teaspoon black pepper
1 bunch green onions (optional)

Dumplings
½ cup cornmeal
¾ cup white flour
2 teaspoons baking powder
½ teaspoon salt
1 tablespoon chicken fat, bacon drippings, or butter
1 egg
½ cup milk
1 teaspoon minced chives, or other green herbs such as marjoram or rosemary

In a large kettle or cauldron with a cover, bring chicken broth to a simmer. Add squirrel and remaining ingredients. Cook until squirrel is tender. (Debone squirrel, if desired, and return to simmering broth.) To make the dumplings, sift together the dry ingredients and cut in the chicken fat, drippings, or butter. Beat together the egg and milk. Stir in the herbs. Mix until just blended. *Do not overmix* or dumplings will be tough. Drop dumpling batter, 1 teaspoon at a time, into the simmering broth and cover. Cook 20 minutes. Serve hot, in bowls.

Dressing the Part

When I look at photos of old-time hunters with their catch, I have to admire their style—good posture, sturdy suit coats, ties, and soft-brim hats. While I'd have a hard time getting through the woods dressed like that, I do have my own hunting uniform of sorts. From the start of pheasant season to the end of rabbit season—some five months—I start with brush pants, a chamois or canvas shirt, and my hunting vest. A base-ball cap keeps the sun out of my eyes. A pair of leather boots with good soles helps me keep my footing in rough country. I jam a water bottle, apple, dog lead, and a dozen shells into the vest, and I'm good to go.

Let me say a word about brush pants—you can choose where you get them but you *must* have a pair or two for serious upland hunting in the thorny covers of the Upper Midwest. You can go with heavy canvas work pants from a farm and home store, or pricier versions from L.L. Bean, Cabela's, Orvis, or Filson. The point is that game likes cover—the nastier the better. Briars, thornapples, barbed wire, brush piles, multi-flora rose—you need to put something between you and the thorns. Jeans just don't cut it, or I should say, jeans get cut up.

When the snows fall, I modify this basic getup. Rubber knee boots slipped inside snowshoes replace leather boots. I put on some thin long johns and a wool stocking cap in place of the baseball cap. (I *do* mean wool; poly-ester doesn't breathe or insulate nearly as well.) Wool socks are a must; even better are wool socks with silk socks worn under them. If you can find a pair of wool pants at a surplus store, you're really in business. With silk worn beneath wool, sweat wicks right off. Next, slip on a mackinaw or Pendleton. And go for gloves over mittens. It's hard to work the safety and trigger wear-ing mittens. The difference between a grouse, pheasant, or rabbit and an empty game pocket often comes down to that extra split second.

Speaking of game, that goes in the back pocket of the hunting vest, or in a canvas gamebag if you don't have a vest. I gut all my game on the spot—allowing the carcass to bleed out and cool before putting it in the vest. If there's grass or cattail handy, I stuff that foliage in the cooled bird or animal to keep dirt out. There are certainly high-tech clothes out there for upland hunters. Go for it as long as it works. But make sure it breathes and keeps you protected from thick cover.

Rabbit Pie

Pies are a welcoming way for the uninitiated to try game. The meat is wrapped in a comforting crust and there are no bones to deal with. Squirrel can be substituted for rabbit here. This is also a clever way to use up leftovers from a venison or gamebird dinner. Just skip the parboiling and use chicken broth in place of rabbit broth.

> 1 cottontail rabbit (or 2 squirrels) cut into serving pieces;
>   or 3 cups diced cooked game meat
> 2 cups broth used for cooking rabbit; 2 cups hot chicken broth
>   if using already-cooked game
> 1 stick of butter
> ¼ cup flour
> 4 shallots, minced
> Dash of sherry or red wine
> 2 tablespoons Italian parsley, chopped
> 1 cup mushrooms, cleaned and sliced
> Salt and pepper to taste
> 1 or 2 9-inch pie crusts (store-bought or home-made)

Cook rabbit until tender in enough salted water to cover. Remove from water, allow to cool, and strip meat from bones. Cook shallots, mushrooms, and parsley in butter until tender; sprinkle with flour, stir, and add hot broth and wine. Stir until smooth. Add salt and pepper to taste and then replace meat. Spoon meat mixture into bottom of 9-inch baking dish and cover with a pie crust. Cut small vents in the crust and crimp edges if you wish. Bake according to crust instructions. If you like a bottom crust on your meat pies, in addition to a top crust, line the dish with it before adding the other ingredients.

Rabbit Creole

A Creole sauce in North American cooking is a tangy, tomato-based concoction enhanced with white wine. More broadly, Creole refers to Old World cultures or languages that have evolved in the New World. Not surprisingly, this sauce shows both New World influence (tomato) as well as Old World (wine and flour thickening). Rabbit does especially well here, though squirrel can be substituted. Use 2 squirrels, as they are about half the size of a rabbit.

1 cottontail rabbit, or 2 squirrels, cut into serving pieces
Flour seasoned with salt and pepper
4 tablespoons peanut oil:
  2 for browning rabbit; 2 for browning vegetables
1 onion, sliced
½ green or red bell pepper, chopped
1 garlic clove, minced
1 cup celery, chopped
28-ounce can of tomatoes, or equivalent in fresh tomatoes
1 cup hot chicken broth
½ cup dry white wine
¼ teaspoon dried thyme
Salt and pepper to taste
Dash of hot sauce, or more to taste

Parboil rabbit for 5 minutes and allow to cool; dredge in seasoned flour; brown in peanut oil in large skillet or Dutch oven; remove to hot platter. In the same pan, brown the onion, pepper, garlic, and celery. Cook until vegetables are soft. Add tomatoes, wine, chicken broth, thyme, salt, pepper, and hot sauce. Replace rabbit. Cook on low flame until tender—about 1½ hours. Serve over cooked white rice.

French Rabbit with Mustard Sauce

This is a nice change of pace from the usual tomato- or mushroom-based sauces that often accompany rabbit. As well as adding sophistication, mustard helps tenderize.

1 cottontail rabbit, cut into serving pieces
Flour seasoned with salt and pepper
4 tablespoons olive oil
4 shallots, finely chopped
¼ teaspoon dried thyme or herbes de Provence
2 cups hot chicken broth
¼ cup Dijon mustard
Salt and pepper to taste

Parboil rabbit for 5 minutes and allow to cool; dredge in seasoned flour; brown in oil in large skillet or Dutch oven; remove to hot platter. In the same pan, gently brown the shallots, adding more oil if necessary. Add herbs, broth, and mustard. Replace rabbit. After dish has cooked for some time, say ½ hour, add salt and pepper to taste. Cook on low flame until tender—a total of about 1½ hours. Serve with steamed green beans, roasted red potatoes, and sourdough bread. Dry white wine or rosé is a good choice to accompany this dish.

HASSENPFEFFER

Rest assured that plenty of German American households in the Upper Midwest have used this Old World rabbit recipe for cottontail rabbit and snowshoe hare. The sourness of the vinegar and sweetness of the cream go well together—and provide a great way to make sure the rabbit is fork-tender.

1 cottontail rabbit or snowshoe hare, skinned
   and cut into serving pieces
1 tablespoon salt
12 allspice berries
10 black peppercorn
1 bay leaf
½ cup vinegar
12 ounces beer
4 tablespoons lard or oil for browning
1 onion, peeled and chopped
Salt and pepper to taste
1 cup sour cream

Place rabbit in the bottom of a large stone bowl or crock. Mix together the next 6 ingredients (the seasonings, vinegar, and beer); pour over rabbit. Refrigerate for 24 hours. Drain rabbit pieces; strain and reserve marinade. In a deep skillet, brown rabbit pieces in hot fat; add reserved liquid and cook rabbit until tender—about 1 hour. Scoop out a cup of cooking liquid and blend it with the sour cream. Add this mixture to the rabbit and cook only until cream is mixed evenly throughout. Serve over egg noodles or dumplings. Pickled red cabbage or baked apples are good side dishes, and beer is the beverage of choice.

Marinated Grilled Rabbit

There is something truly wonderful in the combination of herbs and wild rabbit. Perhaps that's because rabbits do their share of grazing on leafy plants—herbs like wild mint among them—and that flavor is accented here. This recipe is a crowd-pleaser, and elegant in its own way. To avoid charring, cook over coals that have ashed over. Keep the flame low for gas grills. Make sure the grill is well scraped, cleaned, and lightly oiled before cooking.

1 or more cottontail rabbit, cut into serving pieces
Salt and pepper to taste

Marinade
1½ cup dry white wine
½ teaspoon dried thyme
½ teaspoon dried oregano
1 garlic clove, minced
Juice of 1 lemon
¼ cup olive oil
¼ teaspoon black pepper
½ teaspoon salt

Whisk together marinade ingredients. Lightly salt and pepper rabbit pieces. Set in nonreactive container (such as ceramic or glass) and cover with marinade for as little as 4 hours or as long as 24 hours. Grill until tender, turning and basting frequently. Rabbit is done when meat starts to pull away from the bone. Serve with white wine and rice pilaf or pasta. Remaining marinade may be heated for 5 minutes and served with rabbit.

Rabbit with Currants

Currants are a tart bushberry native to northern Europe. A few savvy gardeners in the Upper Midwest grow a patch of them here and there, but they have never really gotten popular on this side of the pond. That's too bad, because they make first-rate jam and provide the perfect counterpoint to game meats. Dried currants, as used in this recipe, are available in the bakery or dried fruit sections of grocery stores. You can find currant jam in most grocery stores.

> 1 cottontail rabbit, cut into serving pieces
> Flour seasoned with salt and pepper
> 4 tablespoons olive oil
> ½ cup dried currants; or equivalent in currant jam
> 1 cup chicken broth
> ½ cup dry white wine
> Salt and pepper to taste

Parboil rabbit for 5 minutes and allow to cool; dredge in seasoned flour; brown in oil in large skillet or Dutch oven; remove to hot platter. To the same pan, add the currants, chicken broth, and wine. Add salt and pepper. Replace rabbit. Cook on low flame until tender—about 1½ hours. Serve over cooked white rice or couscous.

Braised Snowshoe Hare

Knowing how to cook snowshoe hare is a practical thing for folks living in the North-woods. Bag limits and seasons are quite liberal, and there's quite a bit of meat on them—about twice that of a cottontail rabbit. Depending on their age and diet, snowshoe hares can be tender and mild-flavored or a bit tough and gamey. I recommend soaking them in buttermilk overnight or for 24 hours. This will soften the meat and get rid of any strong unwanted flavors. Moist cooking methods—such as stews or braising—are best for hare.

½ gallon buttermilk
1 snowshoe hare, cleaned and cut into pieces
Flour seasoned with salt and pepper
½ cup cooking oil or bacon drippings
1 onion, peeled and chopped
1 carrot, peeled and chopped
1 garlic clove, chopped
1 cup green olives, pitted and chopped
2 cups mushrooms, cleaned and chopped
2 cups red wine
½ teaspoon fresh or dried herbs—parsley, thyme,
    marjoram, oregano
Salt and pepper to taste
Water or broth (if needed)

Marinate hare in buttermilk overnight or for 24 hours. Drain and pat dry. Preheat oven to warm. Dredge in seasoned flour. Heat a large skillet or Dutch oven on the stove-top to medium-hot; add fat and heat until bubbling. Brown hare pieces well; remove browned pieces to a warm oven. Scrape the bottom of pan and brown vegetables, adding more oil or cooking grease if needed. Add wine and herbs; salt and pepper to taste. Replace hare pieces in pan. They should be covered in liquid. If not, add water or broth to cover. Cook, covered, until meat is tender—1½ to 2 hours. Serve over wide egg noodles.

Denny Weiss's Roast Beaver

Denny Weiss works in fisheries research for the Iowa DNR, out of the Bellevue office on the Mississippi River. Denny is also a lifelong trapper and fisherman and gives wildfood cooking demonstrations at the Iowa State Fair. He recommends young beavers between twenty and forty pounds for eating. The back legs have most of the meat, but the front legs and backstrap are also good. Make sure to cut away all fat. When Denny serves roast beaver to guests, they say it tastes as good as roast beef.

> 1 young beaver, skinned and trimmed of fat (4 legs and backstrap)
> Salt and pepper to taste
> 4 cups hot beef broth
> 6 slices of bacon
> 1 onion, peeled and chopped
> 2 carrots, peeled and chopped
> 4 potatoes, peeled and cubed

Preheat oven to 350 degrees. Salt and pepper beaver pieces. Place them in a roasting pan and cover them with bacon slices. Add vegetables and broth. Cook, covered, for 2 hours. Reduce heat to 300 and cook an additional ½ hour. Allow meat to cool. Pull it from the bone. Serve with barbeque sauce or roaster gravy and your choice of potato.

UPLAND BIRDS

Just as species and venues vary for waterfowl hunters across the Upper Midwest, so they do for upland gunners. You might be peering through a screen of green forest and waiting for a wild turkey or pushing out nests of prairie cover on a snowy day as your German shorthair locks up on point. Or perhaps you're waiting over a farm pond on a warm September evening, swatting mosquitoes as the first wave of doves twists in. Maybe you're roaming Northwoods aspen tracts, where blackberry leaves have turned red and a light frost ghosts the grass at your feet. Suddenly the rhythmic clunking of the dog's bell stops, and you wonder whether a woodcock will twitter up or a grouse will rocket from the understory. Yes, there's forest and field; spring, late summer, golden autumn, and snowy winter. And the quarry varies in size from a ½-pound dove to a 20-pound wild turkey.

One could well wax rhapsodic about upland gunning in the Upper Midwest. Many fine writers—Aldo Leopold, Gordon MacQuarrie, Datus Proper, George Harrison, and Thomas McGuane among them—have done just that, and I recommend their work in the highest terms. The task here, however, is somewhat different. A good cookbook must deliver useful information as well as literary flair. So there's work to be done. Or, to be more precise, there's after-the-hunt work to be done, for the hunter has already logged in many miles—to say nothing of briar-scrapes, sunburns, and cold digits—bagging these noble creatures. So from the hunting ground to the kitchen we go. Or, better still, for the kitchen while still in the field we go.

As with waterfowl, there's one cardinal rule that applies to cleaning upland game birds: gut them as soon as possible. This is a simple task, and should be done promptly whether you ultimately plan on skinning or plucking your birds. Pull off a few feathers just below the breastbone and make a small cut parallel to it. Open this vent and remove all entrails. Allow the bird to cool and keep it out of direct sunlight, or place it in your gamebag. Most often, it is impractical to save the hearts and livers of upland birds. But if they are in good condition and can be removed quickly to an ice chest or other cold place, these tasty morsels are well worth adding to dirty rice, grinding into pâté, or using for a game sauce. One exception to the immediate-gutting rule is hunting in below-freezing weather. Here there is no risk of spoilage and the task can wait until you return to home or camp.

Again, as with waterfowl, opinions differ as to whether plucking or skinning is best. Since it is so easy, plucking is the way to go for small game birds—quail, Hungarian partridge, woodcock, and doves. These small parcels take little time—perhaps 5 or 10 minutes per bird—to pluck and the skin adds flavor and moisture. The breast fillets don't add up to much, it seems, but the whole bird is almost a meal. Plucking is also preferable if you plan on whole-roasting larger birds like pheasant or turkey. However, if your recipe calls for a bird cut into pieces—say Pheasant Paprikás—then you might as well save yourself some time and simply skin and joint the bird.

Grouse fall decidedly on the skinning side of this divide. Whether you've bagged ruffed grouse in the northern forests or sharptail grouse on the prairie, you'll find that grouse skin tears easily. Plucking is a frustrating proposition. If your heart is set on roasting skinned grouse, consider placing a strip or two of bacon or salt pork over the breast to keep it moist. Interestingly, ruffed grouse and sharptail grouse have very different tastes. Ruffed grouse have mild white meat while sharptails have darker meat with a more robust taste. While ruffed grouse are easy favorites, opinions differ on the table quality of sharptails. Some hunters enjoy the strong flavor—and pair them with fruit or a marinade—and others do not care for it. I encourage hunters and diners to make up their own minds by actually trying sharptails—or whatever game—carefully cleaned and prepared. Myths are often kept in circulation by repeating what is supposed to be true, instead of what actually is true.

Skinning an upland bird—whether grouse, pheasant, or turkey—takes nothing more than making an incision somewhere in the bird—usually around the breast—and peeling the skin back to the wings. The wings, then, are snipped with a game shears or cut at the first joint, and you are left with a skinless bird. Remember, however, that the law requires gamebirds to have either one wing or the head attached to them when they are being transported.

Freezing upland birds is much the same as freezing waterfowl. You want a tight seal of plastic—accomplished by using a vacuum packer or squeezing excess air from a ziplock—covered in freezer or butcher paper. Label birds with the species and date of harvest. This way you'll know how old they are. Upland birds will keep in the freezer, prepared this way, for about six months. At that point, they lose some of their flavor and can become freezer-burned. Of course, it's best to eat gamebirds the day you bag them, or after they've hung for a spell in cool conditions. Always thaw frozen gamebirds in the refrigerator, not on the countertop. Quick-thawing brings out strong, unwanted flavors.

An interesting note about cooking upland birds: most recipes you use for rabbit will work well for gamebirds. Just cut the birds in parts, skip the parboiling, and brown, braise, stew, or bake as desired. Rabbit with Currants, French Rabbit with Mustard, Rabbit Pie, and Marinated Grilled Rabbit can all be made with pheasant or grouse. Turkey, cut into smaller pieces, will work well. Use two birds if substituting quail or Hungarian partridge.

Turkey, ruffed grouse, and pheasant have similar tastes, especially the breast meat. Similarly, woodcock and doves can take similar treatments, as can quail and Hungarian partridge. Don't hesitate to substitute. Bear in mind, though, that size varies considerably among upland gamebirds. A wild turkey serves four to six, a pheasant two or three, and a ruffed grouse one or two. With ample side dishes, one quail, dove, woodcock, or Hungarian partridge will serve one person.

Upland gamebirds pair well with the sorts of things that accompany turkey or chicken—starches such as stuffing, squash, rice (wild, white, or brown), potatoes, couscous, and cornbread and sharper sides such as cranberry sauce, wine-poached pears, or cinnamon applesauce. If you serve a green salad, add a handful or dried fruit, pecans, or almonds. Wines should be on the lighter end of the spectrum—anything from a pinot noir or Beaujolais to a rosé or dry white like a pinot grigio or sauvignon blanc. Save powerhouses like tempranillos, malbecs, or cabernet sauvignons for venison or waterfowl. As for beer, lagers, pale ales, IPAs, or wheats will all do nicely depending on your taste. Nothing closes out a game meal like fruit pie or cobbler for dessert. If you and your fellow diners don't care for full-on sweets, pass a dish of clementines or mandarins with a few squares of dark chocolate.

Build time into your cooking schedule to give the birds a final cleaning pass. On plucked birds, make sure the cavity is clean of all clotted blood and organ parts. Feel around inside it with your fingers. You should feel nothing but rib bones. If any parts of the bird are badly bloodied or torn up, discard these or use them for stock. For birds with a few embedded pellets, a 1-hour soak in cold salt water will also help draw out the bloody taste. Whether your dinner is a brace of doves bagged over a local farm pond, a limit of pheasant shot on the open prairies, or woodland birds like grouse or turkey, you're in for fine eating.

Whole Roasted Pheasant

That the ringneck pheasant is king of upland birds is a broadly accepted fact among most hunters. In that spirit, this recipe becomes a sort of coronation. For full effect, the bird should be plump, neatly plucked, and free of obvious shot damage. If your freezer has no pheasants in it, you can call, click, or visit a wild game supplier, such as MacFarlane Pheasant Farm, Specialty Meats and Gourmet, or Prairie Harvest.

1 whole pheasant, plucked
Salt, pepper, and poultry seasoning to taste
4 strips of bacon and toothpicks
1 tablespoon butter for sautéing
1 onion, finely chopped
1 apple, skin on, chopped
Small handful of golden raisins
2 cups stale bread cubes or stuffing
12 ounces hot chicken broth

Preheat oven to 325 degrees. Season pheasant inside and out with salt, pepper, and poultry seasoning. Pin bacon strips, two per side, to the breast with toothpicks. Sauté onion and apple in butter; toss with raisins and bread cubes. Loosely stuff bird, add chicken broth to roaster, and cook, covered, for 1 hour or until pheasant is tender. Baste every 15 minutes with pan juices. Serve with candied baked squash, cranberry sauce, and stuffing from the bird.

PHEASANT AVGOLEMONO

This classic Greek chicken-lemon soup works wonderfully with pheasant. The diet of pheasants closely resembles that of the backyard, homegrown chickens originally used to make this dish. As with many Old World recipes, Avgolemono can be stretched this way or that. Made with an entire pheasant, it works as a main meal for two to four. Made with trimmings/leftovers, it serves as a first course. Either way, it is delicious and light on the palate.

> 1 pheasant, skinned and cut into pieces; or any quantity pheasant backs,
>   necks, wingtips; or leftover cooked pheasant
> 1 quart water; if using cooked pheasant, 1 quart chicken broth
> ½ cup uncooked rice
> Salt and pepper to taste
> 3 eggs, beaten
> Juice of 1 lemon
> ¼ teaspoon dried thyme or oregano (optional)

Cook pheasant parts slowly in salted water until they are tender. Remove from water, allow to cool, and strip meat from bone. Return meat to simmering broth and add rice; continue cooking until rice is done. (To make the soup from already-cooked pheasant, add pheasant pieces to hot chicken broth—instead of water—at the same time you add rice. Directions from here are identical.) Add salt and pepper to taste. Add optional herbs; I find that they enhance the dish's flavor. Turn off soup and make sure it has stopped boiling completely. Add lemon juice and stir. To the beaten eggs, add a cup of hot—but not boiling—broth and whisk. Then, whisk egg-broth mixture into soup. Serve hot or cold with crusty bread.

Orange Pheasant

Because gamebirds are usually bagged in fall or winter, pairing them with citrus makes a lot of sense. Produce shelves are full of bright oranges, and their flavor blends very well with the white meat of pheasant or grouse.

1 pheasant or grouse, cut into serving pieces
Flour seasoned with salt and pepper
¼ cup peanut oil
Juice of 2 oranges
2 cups chicken broth
Salt and pepper to taste
Pinch of cinnamon

Dredge bird pieces in seasoned flour; brown them well in a Dutch oven or large skillet. Remove browned pieces to warmed platter and cook orange juice and chicken broth for 5 minutes over medium heat. Replace bird pieces and simmer, covered, until tender—about 1 hour. Serve with rice pilaf and a green or fruit salad.

CHERRY PHEASANT BREASTS

This fine recipe comes from my hunting pal Dan O'Brien. Dan originally developed it for diving ducks shot in Lake Michigan, off Door County, Wisconsin's cherry-growing capital. Over the years, Dan has perfected it. He found that it works equally well for upland birds such as pheasant and grouse.

Fillets from 2 pheasant or grouse
Salt, pepper, and green herbs (thyme or rosemary) to taste
Flour for dredging
2 tablespoons olive oil
2 tablespoons butter
2 minced shallots
1 cup red wine
1 cup chicken broth
Handful of dried pie cherries

Pound breasts—this step is optional, but it serves the double purpose of tenderizing and creating a uniform thickness. Season breasts with salt and pepper and a little thyme or rosemary if desired. Coat breasts in flour (and some cornmeal if desired). Heat olive oil over medium-high heat in a pan just big enough for the quantity of breasts. Fry breasts in oil, flipping once, so they are nicely browned and cooked through. Remove to paper-towel-lined plate; cover with foil and keep warm. Add butter to the pan, and sauté shallots. Once shallots are softened and starting to brown, add red wine and dried cherries. Increase heat to high and reduce sauce by half, stirring frequently. To serve, spoon cherries over breasts, and drizzle with pan sauce. Sauerkraut and skin-on mashed potatoes are great side dishes for this special meal.

Pheasant Paprikás

A staple of Hungarian cooking, paprikás is a slow-cooked dish containing meat, onions, paprika, sour cream, and sometimes tomatoes and peppers. It's usually made with chicken or pork, but pheasant adds an interesting twist—and flavor. Rather than masking the gamebird's taste, paprika and the tangy sauce actually enhance it. One caution (and I know all Hungarian cooks will agree): Don't burn the onions! If you do, start over and remove any burnt onion from the pan.

> 1 pheasant, skinned and cut into serving pieces
> Flour seasoned with salt and pepper
> 4 tablespoon lard or olive oil, plus more if needed
> 1 large onion, finely chopped
> ½ green bell pepper or several wax peppers, chopped and seeded
> 1 large tomato, chopped
> 1 cup chicken broth
> 1 tablespoon Hungarian paprika, sweet or hot
> Salt and pepper to taste
> 2 tablespoons additional flour
> 1 cup sour cream

Dredge pheasant pieces in seasoned flour. In a large skillet or cauldron—whatever vessel you're using must have a lid—heat the lard or olive oil. When it's hot, but not smoking, drop in the pheasant pieces a few at a time, being careful not to crowd the pan; remove them to a warm platter when browned. Sauté the onion in the remaining drippings; add more drippings if necessary. When onion is translucent, add the tomato, pepper, and paprika. Cook until the tomato pieces release their juices, then add the hot broth and replace the pheasant parts. Cook, covered, over low flame for 1 hour, or until pheasant pieces are tender. Check seasoning and add salt and pepper to taste. Remove a few ounces of cooking liquid and whisk it together with additional flour; add sour cream and stir to make a paste. Add this paste to the paprikás and stir so that it mixes evenly. Cook on lowest flame until sauce begins to thicken. Serve over egg noodles or mashed potatoes with a green salad and rosé wine.

Oyster Mushrooms
with Pheasant Breasts

If your pheasant hunting, like mine, takes you into the river bottom country, you have a good chance of finding oyster mushrooms. This tasty fungus grows from summer to early winter in moist areas. Look for them on downed deciduous trees and harvest young, soft mushrooms because these make the best eating. You might at first have trouble seeing oysters, since their neutral color (buff, gray, or light yellow) blends with downed wood. But after some practice your eye will be drawn to their shape. As with any wild mushroom, eat only those that you can positively identify.

There's no truth, by the way, to the idea that oyster mushrooms taste like seafood. The name comes from the shape of the mushroom, which resembles an oyster shell. If you don't find oyster mushrooms, take heart. Commercial growing of specialty mushrooms is becoming more common each year. You can buy oyster mushrooms at larger supermarkets, natural food co-ops, and at farm markets.

Breast fillets from 1 pheasant, sliced into 1-inch ribbons
Flour seasoned with salt and pepper
Thyme to taste
4 tablespoons butter
½ pound oyster mushrooms, sliced
3 shallots, chopped
2 cups chicken or pheasant broth

Clean oyster mushrooms of any debris with a damp cloth or paper towel. Heat large skillet and melt butter. Dredge pheasant pieces in flour; shake off excess. Quickly brown pheasant pieces—they should be crisp on the outside and still pink on the inside—and remove them to a warm platter. Sauté mushrooms and shallots in remaining pan drippings; sprinkle with thyme. Add more butter if needed. Add broth and simmer until reduced by half. Replace pheasant pieces and cook until just done—do not overcook. Serve over pasta or rice.

Farm-Raised Game

In his *Meditations on Hunting*, Spanish philosopher Ortega y Gasset famously wrote that wild game, by its nature, is scarce—there's always a limited supply. Ortega y Gasset often gets credit for this idea, but, really, he's giving voice to something known to hunters for thousands of years. There'd be no pictographs of game animals chiseled into rock, elaborate ceremonies before the hunt, or long blank stretches in the deer stand and duck blind if this wasn't true. While the contents of your gamebag will always be uncertain, getting your favorite game meat doesn't have to be. The Upper Midwest has a number of businesses devoted to producing quality game for the table—both birds and big game.

One such business is MacFarlane Pheasant Farm, located just north of the Illinois border in Janesville, Wisconsin. MacFarlane is the largest producer of pheasants in the United States. Most of the birds here go to hunting preserves, but some are raised for food. I was interested to learn on a visit to MacFarlane that their "eater" birds are a different strain of pheasant known as white pheasants. Housed in large pens enclosed by netting, these birds feed on corn and soybeans as well as wild plants such as lamb's quarter. MacFarlane birds are more forgiving in the oven than leaner wild birds, but are still low in fat and have that distinctive pheasant taste. High-end restaurants in Chicago, New York, Las Vegas, and Colorado buy the lion's share of MacFarlane table birds. In fact, according to CEO Bill MacFarlane, the vast majority of pheasants in U.S. restaurants comes from MacFarlane. They do a brisk online business—also offering quail, rabbit, and venison—and you can also buy birds from the freezer case in the gift shop of the Janesville store.

Further north, in the heart of the Upper Midwest on the Minnesota border in Hudson, Wisconsin, you'll find Specialty Meats and Gourmet.

Specialty started in 1990 as an outlet for local deer farmers, and venison raised on small farms in Minnesota and Wisconsin is still the focus. How does Specialty venison compare to the deer you might shoot on opening day? Just as farm-raised pheasant is moister than wild pheasant, so farm-raised venison is more tender than wild venison. Translation: they're easier to cook because their lives—ready access to food and water, lack of predators—are easier. Specialty now carries a wide variety of game—including wild boar, antelope, elk, bison, and gamebirds. Like MacFarlane, they sell both online and through their store in their headquarters building. Other suppliers/producers in the region include Blackwing Ostrich Farms in Antioch, Illinois, and Prairie Harvest in Spearfish, South Dakota.

Next time you come home from a hunt empty-handed, don't despair. A wild game dinner is just a click or call away.

Grilled Small Gamebirds

Dan O'Brien and his Brittany spaniel Ida are first-rate woodcock hunters. Dan's simple recipe, below, lets the woodcock's earthy flavor come through. Just about any small gamebird—quail, dove, or Hungarian partridge—can be used here. Breast fillets from pheasants or wild turkey will also work; make sure to allow extra cooking time for them.

Any number of plucked woodcock, doves, quail,
**   or Hungarian partridge**
Salt, pepper, and thyme to taste
½ lemon
Olive oil
1 clove garlic per bird (optional)

Rub bird generously inside and out with cut lemon; season inside and out with salt, pepper, and thyme. Stuff garlic clove inside bird, if desired. Brush bird with olive oil and let bird rest for at least ½ hour, so flavors can penetrate. Preheat gas grill to 350 degrees. If cooking with charcoal, allow briquettes to ash over. Cook birds 5 minutes on each side. They should be crisp on the outside and juicy on the inside. Do not overcook. Serve one bird per person for a light dinner. Couscous, rice, mashed potatoes, or crusty French bread are good sides.

Gamebirds au Vin

Wisconsin hunter Dan O'Brien spends autumns in a state of dizzying flight—up to the Northwoods to pursue ruffed grouse and woodcock, out to the prairies to chase pheasants and sharptails, and back to Wisconsin's marshes to make life miserable for the ducks. Dan gets a lot of birds, and his recipes are camp-tested. "It's like coq au vin with gamebirds," Dan says of this recipe. It's his go-to for pheasant or grouse. While the bird does get nice and tender, the real draw may be the rich gravy that builds up. You'll need a Dutch oven or other large, lidded vessel that can go from stovetop to oven.

> 1 pheasant or grouse cut into serving pieces
> 2 strips of bacon
> Salt, pepper, and thyme to taste
> 1 cup finely diced onion, carrot, and celery
> ½ cup finely diced mushrooms
> 2 tablespoons flour
> 1 cup red wine
> 1 cup water

Season bird pieces well with salt, pepper, and thyme. Cook bacon in the bottom of casserole, and reserve bacon; brown bird pieces in drippings. When browned, remove them and add vegetables; cook until wilted, adding cooking oil or additional bacon drippings if needed. Add mushrooms and cook briefly. Dust vegetables with flour and stir, then add wine and water. Cook for 5 minutes. Add reserved bacon strips, which have been diced. Nestle bird pieces into gravy and cook, covered, until fork-tender—about 1 to 1½ hours—in a 350-degree oven. To serve, arrange bird pieces on a platter and cover with sauce, which may be strained if you want a finer presentation. Mashed potatoes, wild rice, and polenta are all good sides for this robust dish. You'll want to have plenty of crusty bread on hand, and a good store of red wine to wash it all down.

QUAIL À LA BUD

When my sister Christina married into the Smith family of St. Louis, Missouri, I had the good fortune of meeting her father-in-law, Bud. Bud was a big outdoorsman in his day, and he remembers growing up outside of St. Louis in the 1940s. "It didn't take long to get out in the country then," he says. Bud has had many hunting companions over the years, but his favorite was a big English pointer he hunted with as a boy. Bud was the dog's name, and according to family lore, the dog was Bud Smith's namesake. This recipe is a tribute to both Buds—and the idea that simple can be best.

**Any quantity of plucked quail or doves (1 per person as
    a light main course, less for an appetizer)
Salt and pepper to taste
2 tablespoons bacon drippings, or more as needed
Water**

Salt and pepper birds inside and out. In a heavy iron skillet, melt the drippings and brown birds on both sides. Add water to keep pan moist and cook until birds are fork-tender—between 30 and 45 minutes. Serve with cooked greens and cornbread.

Mango Wild Turkey

This is one of the endless variations on the theme of fruit and fowl. Here, the mix of mango and chili leans toward Latin America. If you like heat, add a few more dried chili peppers. The sweet and spicy sauce that cooks down with the turkey is a nice change of pace from heavier European game recipes.

Breast of 1 wild turkey, cut into strips
Salt, pepper, and chili powder to taste
½ cup flour
½ cup cornmeal
¼ cup peanut oil
2 dried chilies, or more to taste
1 red onion, sliced
1 small handful of cilantro, chopped
Additional salt

Season wild turkey pieces with salt, pepper, and chili powder; roll in flour-corn-meal mixture. Heat oil in a heavy, lidded casserole and brown the turkey; when brown, add the onion, mango, cilantro, and chilies. Cover and cook on low for 1 hour or until the turkey pieces are tender. Take off lid during last 15 minutes of cooking to thicken. Serve with pico de gallo, black beans, white rice, and cornbread or corn tortillas. Cold Mexican beer with lime slices, or sangria, will help set the mood.

WATERFOWL

The scenarios for waterfowl hunting are so varied across the Upper Midwest that a number of pictures need to be painted, if only to pay homage to the breadth of opportunities, before we get down to the business of cleaning and eating.

Imagine yourself ensconced on a rocky Great Lakes island. Three dozen decoys roll on the metal-gray water as the veil of morning is beginning to part. A stiff wind blows from the north and brings with it the smell of cold. As with so many moments in the sporting world, you hear it before you see it—the sound, like that of ripping canvas, of an approaching squadron of diving ducks. The big, square-headed Chesapeake Bay retriever beside you begins to whimper. You grip the stock of your shotgun—*Yes, they're coming*—and rise to knock down two big, gray-backed redheaded ducks. Your retriever is already off after the first bird, as you wade to the water's edge to get the second. Already, you're thinking of stopping by the farm stand on the way back to the cottage for a package of dried cherries to cook with these ducks and perhaps a squash or two to have on the side.

Or maybe you are lying, face to mud, in a cut cornfield. Light snow is falling. The lines of trees and hedge separating the surrounding farms have lost their leaves, and there is something like melancholy in the air. You hear the far-off calls of geese, and then see them moving, the groups undulating and amoeba-like against the leaden sky. Too, there are high, tight clouds of mallards moving and every now and again you hear chuckles from above. If there were a message written across the sky, it would be something like, "Store up. Cold is coming." Cold is *coming*? "Hell no," you think, shifting positions to get feeling back in your limbs, "cold is here!" As you're occupied with matters of linguistics and bodily comfort, you notice something big lumbering toward you. The morning's first goose! You rear up on your knees, shouldering the old doublegun, and manage to knock it down on the second shot.

And then there are those duckweed-thick sloughs a few miles from the Mississippi River. You park at the fairground lot and there is a light frost on the grass. Hip boots and a handful of shells are all you need—that and the lithe black Labrador retriever that springs from her kennel in the back of your pickup truck. "Quiet, girl," you say, patting her head. "Quiet, girl." The two of you pad down the sand path. A pair of wood ducks perched on a log see you and whistle off, breaking the morning calm. But no matter. You're sneaking around to a pond of flooded pin oaks. It takes some pains on both your parts to ignore the big gray squirrel mewing in the tree, but then you round the corner. Your dog's chocolate eyes are fixed on you. Her whimper causes a cluster of wood ducks to take wing. You manage to take a departing drake, which she retrieves, crying with happiness.

And then there's the beginning of prairie pothole country in western Minnesota and Iowa. You've closed the screen door on the farmhouse you're renting. No need to start the truck—there's a hidden little pothole just a quarter-mile away, beyond the hay bales. The night sky is giving way to morning, and in that changing of the guard, the wild-fowl have begun to announce themselves. There's the deep rattle of sandhill cranes. The high-pitched yelping of snow geese. And the muffled *quack-a-ack-ack* of puddle ducks. Slipping beneath the swale, you see the morning flight has begun and you take cover. A pair of gadwall is headed right for you and you rise up and shoot.

Now, this could go for some time longer—navigating wild rice marshes, gunning the wide expanses of the Mississippi and Missouri rivers, jump-shooting secret forest streams of the Northwoods—but there's business at hand. And that is getting down to the cooking of these unique and wonderful birds. It may seem a paradox to some that a hunter could love his quarry so much and yet still seek to bring it to his larder. But that, like the farmer who shepherds his flock but still culls it, is a paradox we will have to live with. And so on to the cleaning and cooking of waterfowl.

You may know—or have picked up—the words *puddle duck* and *diving duck* in the previous paragraphs. This is as good a place to start as any. Puddle ducks pursued by hunters are shallow-water feeders, like the mallards you see in the city park with their butts tipped up, only wild and skittish. The word *puddle* is a hint at their habitat—shallow water. As shallow-water feeders, this class of ducks eats mostly aquatic plants that they can reach easily by extending their necks down into the water or pecking at the surface. Wild rice, duckweed, and other pondweeds are favorite foods of puddle ducks. Puddle ducks are quite adept on land, too—able to forage for acorns and grapes in the woods and very fond of picked grainfields as well. Since their diet is mainly vegetable matter, they make for prime eating. Plucking, as you would for a chicken, is the best way to prepare these birds for the table. The skin helps keep in moisture and flavor. There is something very pretty, too, about a whole plucked wild duck browned crisp for the table.

Puddle ducks range in size from the diminutive teal—not much bigger than a dove or pigeon—to a three-pound, wild-rice-fattened mallard or black duck. Wood duck, wigeon, gadwall, and shoveler are what one might call medium-sized puddle ducks, weighing in between one and two pounds. All of these ducks make for prime eating. An exception to this is the shoveler, which consumes a higher proportion of animal matter (plankton and freshwater shrimp), siphoning them through the "teeth" of their long spatula-like bills. But even shoveler, countered with a high-acid fruit such as cherries or oranges, makes for decent eating. The others have a distinctive combination of lean meat and rich flavor, not unlike a fine beef roast.

Diving ducks, as the Great Lakes vignette above illustrates, tend to frequent large bodies of water. Just as puddle ducks tip up their butts and extend their necks down into the water to feed, so diving ducks—as their name implies—propel themselves down into the water column by means of their feet and short, powerful wings. As such, they are prone to feed lower in the water and are more likely to consume crustaceans and mollusks as part of their diet. Scaup, goldeneye, and bufflehead are diving ducks whose diet consists, in the main, of animal matter. In fact, the word *scaup* derives from the Gaelic word for mollusk or scallop. The diving ducks, then, tend to have a stronger flavor, and are best made kitchen-ready by filleting out the breast and saving the legs for another use, such as pie or pâté. Like the shoveler, these stronger-flavored ducks do well with high-acid fruits and marinades. To make matters a bit more confusing, some diving ducks eat a sizable amount of plant matter—mainly the tubers of submerged vegetation such as wild celery and sago pondweed. These are the canvasback, redhead, and ringneck. Plucking, as for puddle ducks, is the preferred method of cleaning these prime eaters.

Geese are similar to puddle ducks in terms of food preference and feeding style—that is, they feed while in the water with their butts tipped up and they eat mostly vegetable matter. In fact, given their druthers, they feed in grainfields, where they can easily pack on calories to fuel their big bodies as they make their journey southward. Cut corn, wheat, soybeans, and oats are favorites of wild geese. And they will gobble down wild rice, as will any wild duck, with abandon. While Canada geese are by far the most common among geese in the Upper Midwest, others do show up, especially in western Minnesota and along the Missouri River in western Iowa. These are the snow goose and whitefronted goose. Wild geese, being grain-feeders, are all well-flavored. The challenge lies in keeping them moist, which can be done by means of slow, moist roasting or marinating the breast and cooking them medium-rare.

If I have moved too quickly over the terms "plucked" and "breasted" or "filleted out," perhaps some elaboration is in order. By "plucking," I mean removing feathers. This is pretty much a matter of pulling handfuls of plumage and being careful not to break the skin. Often this is done in the field, where left-behind feathers or viscera are not an issue. Some folks dunk them briefly in paraffin or boiling water with a touch of dish soap. The paraffin is allowed to cool, and then peeled off. Ducks dunked in boiling water should be plucked while still hot. Both of these techniques aid in removing small pinfeathers. And it's worth noting that plucking a goose is much more of a commitment—perhaps an hour or more—than a duck, which is more of a 15-minute chore.

Heads and feet are snipped off with a kitchen or game shears or a sharp knife. Wings are sheared at the first joint. Venting—that is, removing of entrails, heart, and liver—should take place in the field. Intact livers and hearts—those not tinged by shot—work well in pâté and dirty rice, so set these aside in a cooler or refrigerator. There is always a second pass of plucking, and this becomes something of a cost-benefit analysis: how much time do I want to spend and how much better am I going to get it? Useful tools for this second pass are a Scripto lighter and tweezers for stubborn pinfeathers. No matter how much time you spend, though, your duck or goose is not likely to look like a grocery store chicken.

Breasting out or filleting is an easier proposition. You make a small cut near the top of the breast and peel the skin back, exposing lean, red meat. Then, one cut is made on either side of, and along, the breastbone. Be careful here; this is good meat and you want as much as possible on the fillets. The second cut is made where the breast meets the wing—essentially around and over this joint. You can also snip the wing bone with a shears. Now, bring the cut down to the end of the rib cage and keep "peeling" the meat from the breastbone. You should end up with two fillets. Again, strong-flavored ducks such as shoveler, scaup, goldeneye, and bufflehead should be breasted out. Geese are sometimes breasted out, as well, because determining their age (and thus tenderness) is difficult, and it is easier to make breast fillet tender than it is for a whole goose.

On geese and larger ducks, it is worthwhile filleting out the drumsticks. These can be used in a pâté, spaghetti sauce, soup, gumbo, or stock. When transporting ducks and geese, the head or one fully feathered wing must be left on. This is to comply with state and federal migratory bird regulations.

With plucking or breasting behind us, we're pretty close to table-ready. The last decision to make is whether to freeze your ducks and geese or eat them right away. Cleaned ducks and geese will last about a week in the refrigerator, and they actually get more tender as they age. While it's nice to save gamebirds for a big dinner, the flavors in fresh duck and goose are brighter fresh than frozen. So you'll have to decide whether to delay the pleasure or eat them as they come. I tend to do a bit of each. The main thing to keep in mind about freezing waterfowl—as with all game and fish to be frozen—is to prevent air space. Commercial vacuum sealers work well, but a ziplock-wrapped bird sheathed in butcher paper is nearly as good. Allow two days in the refrigerator for proper thawing. Prior to cooking, give your ducks and geese a soak in cold salt water for an hour or two. This helps get rid of any undesirable flavor and helps tenderize the bird.

While a whole flock of recipes follows, the truism that fruit goes well with wild game reaches its fullest expression with wildfowl. Applesauce, cranberry sauce, stewed plums or cherries—even fruit roasted right inside the bird—you can't go wrong with fruit and fowl. You don't need anything fancy for a starch—garlic mashed potatoes, egg noodles, or basmati rice will do the trick. Waterfowl demands heft from a red wine in the same way that venison does. Go for an aged Tempranillo, Cabernet, or Bordeaux.

Simple Roasted Duck

While there's much to be said for fruit sauces and mushroom gravies, sometimes it's best to let the flavor of game speak for itself. This is especially true for young, tender ducks shot during the early season. But any prime-eating duck will do.

Any quantity of plucked puddle ducks, or choice diving ducks
    such as canvasback, redhead, or ringneck
1 garlic clove, cut in half
Salt and pepper to taste
Melted butter

Preheat oven to 400 degrees. Rub ducks with cut garlic clove. Salt and pepper them inside and out, then brush with melted butter. Place birds in a broiler pan or roaster and cook on one side, then flip and cook on the other side. For small ducks like teal, allow 10 to 12 minutes per side for medium-rare; for larger ducks, allow 15 to 18 minutes per side. The breast meat will be like fine, rare steak. The thighs will require a bit of chewing, but the lighter meat there is also prime and tasty. Serve with robust red wine and green salad.

Halved Boneless Duck

This recipe involves a different way of cleaning wild duck, then marinating and quick cooking. Begin with a whole, plucked duck and cut it in half at the breastbone. Next, turn the duck halves meat-side-up on a cutting board or other flat surface and cut out the rib bones and backbone. Cut off what remains of the breastbone on the two duck halves. While this recipe features a marinade, dry-rub methods—including Cajun seasoning, fine herbs plus salt and pepper, or even curry powder—are also good. When using this recipe, note that halved duck cooks much more quickly than whole, bone-in birds.

**Any quantity of prime-eating ducks, halved and boned
    as described above
Salt, pepper, and thyme to taste
2 tablespoons butter for skillet cooking, or more as needed**

Marinade
**1 cup of sherry or Marsala wine
3 tablespoons currant jam
1 garlic clove, diced
¾ teaspoon salt
¼ teaspoon black pepper**

Season both sides of the duck halves with salt, pepper, and thyme. Make marinade by combining remaining ingredients; whisk or stir together. This amount of marinade will be sufficient for 1 or 2 ducks. Place ducks in nonreactive container (such as stainless steel, food-grade plastic, or stoneware) and cover with marinade. Marinate, covered, in the refrigerator for 1 to 4 hours. Grill or flash-cook in a skillet with butter. Serve half a duck per person. For small ducks, such as teal, serve two halves per person.

MUSHROOM-ROASTED DUCK

Mushrooms bring out the deep, rich undertones in game. Buttons and portabella mushrooms work well in this classic duck recipe, but you might want to kick it up a notch with more exotic varieties. Maybe you found a handful of oyster mushrooms growing from a log on the way out of the marsh. Maybe you want to rehydrate those morels in Mason jars above your stove. You can also buy a variety of mushrooms—such as shiitake and oyster—in the grocery store. Avoid using strong-tasting ducks such as bufflehead, scaup, or shoveler in this recipe and go for prime-eating puddlers, or divers such as canvasback, redhead, or ringneck.

Any quantity of choice plucked ducks
Salt, pepper, and thyme to taste
2 tablespoons butter per duck plus more for final browning
¼ pound fresh mushrooms per duck
1 tablespoon flat leaf parsley per duck
1 minced garlic clove per duck
2 cups beef broth
½ cup red wine
Flour or cornstarch for gravy

Preheat oven to 300 degrees. Generously season duck inside and out with salt, pepper, and thyme. Heat a large skillet and melt butter in it. Brown ducks well on both sides. Remove ducks breast side down to a roasting pan. Brown garlic, parsley, and mushrooms in drippings that remain in skillet, or add more butter as necessary; deglaze skillet with broth and wine and pour over ducks. Cover roaster and cook for 2 hours. If breasts are not brown at this point, turn the ducks over and brush with butter. Turn oven up to 400 degrees and brown for an additional 15 minutes. Separate out fat from roasting juices, and thicken the latter with flour or cornstarch to make gravy. If using dried mushrooms, soak them in water as you skillet-brown the ducks; add the reconstituted mushrooms in place of fresh ones and use mushroom water in bottom of roasting pan.

Morel Mushroom Stroganoff

While Stroganoff is commonly thought of as Russian, its origins—julienned meat and vegetables—speak of the nineteenth-century French chefs who served it to the Stroganoff family. In any case, the lean meat of duck or goose breast works well in place of the traditional beef. If you're trying to get your head around how to cook this dish, think stir-fry rather than stew or goulash. Since the cooking is quick, the meat must be tender— thus the long marinating. The addition of morel mushrooms—which many wildfood enthusiasts keep dried for just such an occasion—adds an Upper Midwestern twist to this Eastern European standby. If you're lucky enough to have a batch of fresh morels on hand and duck or goose in the freezer, skip the directions for reconstituting dried mushrooms.

2 pounds duck breast or goose breast cut across the grain
   into inch-wide strips
1 large onion, sliced
2 garlic cloves, minced
1 ounce dried morel mushrooms (or 1 cup fresh mushrooms)
¼ cup vegetable oil
1 cup sour cream
Flat leaf parsley, chopped

Marinade
1 cup sherry, port, or Marsala wine
1 teaspoon sugar
¼ cup vegetable oil
½ teaspoon black pepper
1 teaspoon salt

The night before you prepare this dish, combine marinade ingredients and whisk together. Salt and pepper meat; place in a nonreactive container and add marinade. Allow to marinate overnight. The next day, as you begin cooking, soak dried mushrooms in water; when they are reconstituted, chop them coarsely. Drain the meat through a colander and reserve the marinade. Heat oil in a wok or large skillet on the stovetop. Cook the meat until just done (as you would for stir-fry). Remove with a slotted spoon and keep warm. Sauté garlic, onion, and mushroom, adding additional cooking oil if needed. Add reserved marinade and mushroom liquid. Cook for 10 minutes. Turn off heat, thoroughly stir in sour cream, replace meat, and serve. Traditional accompaniments are mashed potatoes or egg noodles. Garnish with chopped flat leaf parsley.

CURRANT ROASTED DUCK

Native to northern Europe, currants have been slow to catch on in America. That's a pity because they grow well in Northern Tier states and have a truly distinctive flavor. I grow just enough each year for jam and flavoring vodka. To allow the flavor to really penetrate, I use duck breast here and reserve the drumsticks for another use. While this recipe brings out the bright flavors in mallard and teal, it also moderates the stronger taste of bluebill, goldeneye, and shoveler.

Breast fillets from 2 large ducks or 4 small ducks
Salt and pepper to taste
½ stick of butter

Marinade
4 tablespoons currant jam
1 cup dry red wine
2 chopped shallots
¼ cup peanut oil
1 teaspoon salt
¼ teaspoon black pepper
¼ teaspoon thyme

Salt and pepper duck breasts. Mix together marinade ingredients; pour over duck into nonreactive vessel. Allow to marinate, covered, in the refrigerator for 1 to 4 hours. Remove duck breasts from the marinade and pat dry. Reserve marinade. Heat butter in a large skillet. Cook breasts quickly in hot butter—3 minutes per side for large ducks and 2 minutes per side for small ducks. Cook reserved marinade, vigorously, in skillet for 5 minutes. Pour over duck breasts. Serve with wild rice and crusty bread.

Canvasback with Celery

The notion that one is what one eats is often applied to humans. The same can be said of wild game. For instance, the Latin name of canvasback ducks, *valisinera*, refers to the water celery plant on which this large and regal duck feeds. No surprise, then, that celery pairs so well with canvasback and the host of other wild ducks that eat it. It's worth noting for hunters and birders alike that nearly half of the continental population of canvasbacks (some 300,000 at the height of migration) mass together on the Upper Mississippi River on the Wisconsin-Iowa-Minnesota border. In late October and early November, they can be seen diving for wild celery right from the public spotting scope in the small river town of Ferryville, Wisconsin. Nearly extirpated by market hunters who sold these choice ducks by the barrel to big city restaurants, the canvasback has now returned to stable population levels thanks to the hard work of state, federal, and private conservation efforts.

> 2 plucked canvasback ducks (or other large, prime-eating ducks
>   such as mallard or pintail)
> Salt, pepper, and poultry seasoning to taste
> 2 tablespoons butter for browning, or more as needed
> 4 celery stalks
> 1 onion, quartered
> 1 apple, quartered
> 1 quart hot chicken broth

Preheat oven to 250 degrees. Season the ducks inside and out with salt, pepper, and poultry seasoning. In a large skillet, or two smaller ones, brown the ducks well on both sides in melted butter. Allow them to cool and then stuff their cavities with celery, onion, and apple. Place breast side down in a roasting pan; add the chicken broth. Cook, covered, for 2½ hours or until meat falls from the bone. Discard stuffing from cavity. Cut the ducks up and place them on a serving platter. Wild rice or mashed potatoes and homemade applesauce are good sides.

DUCK GUMBO

There are lots of good reasons to make gumbo. One that gets right to the spirit of this catchall Cajun dish is stretching the day's bag to make a camp meal. Another is because it warms body and soul. Still another is just because . . . just because it's damned good eating with some crusty French bread and cold beer. What follows is more a basic guideline than a hard-and-fast recipe. Chicken, rabbit, squirrel, shrimp, crab, catfish, and okra are other common add-ins.

1 duck, squirrel, or rabbit
2 quarts water
2 celery stalks, diced
1 onion, chopped
2 garlic cloves, minced
½ bell pepper, diced
1 pound smoked ham or spicy sausage
14-ounce can tomatoes
1 bay leaf
1 teaspoon thyme
Salt, pepper, and hot sauce to taste

Roux
4 tablespoons peanut oil or lard
4 tablespoons flour

Simmer game slowly in large pot until meat falls from the bone; reserve broth. Remove meat and allow to cool. In a large heavy-bottom kettle, cook the flour and grease (the roux) together slowly. Do not let them burn, but stir constantly over the lowest flame possible. Add celery, onion, garlic, and bell pepper; cook until wilted. If you find the vegetables just are not browning, add some water. Add reserved broth, tomatoes, bay leaf, ham/sausage, and spices. Cook for 1 hour, stirring occasionally, and adjusting seasonings to make sure it has at least some heat when it hits the tongue—how much is up to you. Ladle gumbo over cooked rice bowls. Serve with crusty French bread, ice-cold beer, and let the good times roll.

DUCK AND BARLEY SOUP

Part of hunting is watching the grand spectacle unfold. I've had the pleasure of observing spiraling flocks of mallard and pintail feeding in the grainfields of North Dakota. One evening, after shooting hours were over, wave after wave of wildfowl came in to feed in the harvested barley fields near the town of Bremen. Watching them was every bit as satisfying as hunting. As I sat with my back against the remains of an old duck blind, the food part of my brain got to thinking about duck and barley, duck and barley, and there seemed nothing more natural than making a soup of those ingredients. I tried it and was pleased with results. The taste here is like that of beef-barley soup, but the wild duck flavor adds another dimension.

1 large or 2 small wild puddle ducks, plucked or skinned
1 gallon of water
2 tablespoons butter
1 onion, sliced
1 garlic clove, minced
1 cup mushrooms, sliced
2 carrots, peeled and sliced
1 bay leaf
½ teaspoon thyme
½ cup barley
½ teaspoon salt
¼ teaspoon pepper

First, cook duck slowly in water until meat is tender. Remove duck from water (keeping water on a low flame) and, once cooled, strip duck meat from bones. In a separate heavy skillet, brown the onion, garlic, mushrooms, and carrot in butter. Add browned vegetables and duck meat to the hot broth. Add also the barley, thyme, salt, pepper, and bay leaf. Cook 1 hour and serve with dark bread and green salad. This soup is as good or better the next day.

DIRTY RICE

Dirty rice is one of those wonderful dishes that can be expanded to include nearly anything in your refrigerator—or gamebag—including waterfowl liver or hearts. Use only game hearts and livers that are unpenetrated by shot; put them in the fridge or on ice as soon as possible. Other things that can go in dirty rice are leftover cooked game meat, chicken livers, ham or sausage, and garden vegetables including tomatoes, beans, and zucchini.

> **Hearts and livers from several ducks or geese**
> **(or 1 pound of chicken liver), coarsely chopped**
> **3 tablespoons bacon fat or cooking oil**
> **1 onion, chopped**
> **2 garlic cloves, minced**
> **1 green or red bell pepper, chopped**
> **2 celery stalks, including leaves, minced**
> **1 bay leaf**
> **½ teaspoon thyme**
> **2 cups hot chicken broth or wine**
> **3 cups cooked rice (approximately 1 cup raw rice**
> **that has been cooked according to standard recipe)**
> **Dash of hot sauce, or more to taste**
> **Salt and pepper to taste**

Brown livers and hearts in bacon drippings or oil. Add onion, garlic, bell pepper, and celery. Cook until onion wilts. Add bay leaf and thyme. Add hot broth or wine—this can be added earlier if more moisture is needed while vegetables are browning—then add rice and cook until some of the liquid is absorbed (it can be as dry or moist as you like). Season with hot sauce, salt, and pepper to taste. Dirty rice makes a fun and hearty side dish to any meal of game, especially waterfowl. You can also douse it with pan gravy from your main meat course.

Fancy Duck Liver Sauce

This colonial-era duck recipe is both frugal in its use of duck liver and somehow elegant and restrained. Stray backs or necks can be included here to make the sauce even richer. The only caveat is to use livers that are intact (free of shot damage) and cooled soon after the bird was killed.

Neck and/or back of choice puddle duck
    (mallard, teal, wigeon, gadwall, pintail, or black duck)
Duck liver(s)
2 cups water or chicken broth
1 tablespoon chopped onion
1 garlic clove, minced
2 ounces red wine
1 ounce brandy
1 tablespoon green olives, minced
2 mushrooms, diced
2 tablespoons flour, sifted

Place duck parts, including liver, in broth or water and cook ½ hour. Remove duck parts and discard; chop liver and return to broth. Add onion, garlic, red wine, brandy, olives, and mushrooms and cook another 10 minutes. Add sifted flour, stirring, over low heat until sauce reaches desired consistency. Serve over French bread rounds or on buttered toast.

WILD RICE GOOSE

Wild rice and waterfowl are closely connected. In the marsh, ducks and geese feed heavily on this high-protein food. The tall stalks also provide nesting and loafing cover. In the kitchen, the tastes go together beautifully. Wild rice brings out the characteristic dark flavor of waterfowl. This pairing is enhanced here by the addition of mushrooms and sausage.

1 Canada, snow, or whitefront goose, plucked (or equivalent
   in choice-eating ducks like mallard, teal, wood duck, or ringneck)
Salt, pepper, and poultry seasoning to taste
1 cup dry wild rice prepared according to package directions
¼ pound uncased breakfast sausage
6 breakfast sausage links
1 onion, minced
1 cup button or other mushrooms
2 cups beef broth, heated

Preheat oven to 300 degrees. Generously season goose inside and out with salt and pepper and poultry seasoning. Brown loose sausage in skillet. Cook onions and mushrooms in sausage drippings until soft. In a large bowl, mix onion, mushroom, and sausage with cooked wild rice. Stuff cavity of goose loosely with this mixture and reserve additional rice stuffing for another use. Pin sausage links to the breast of the goose with toothpicks. Pour broth into the bottom of a large roasting pan and place goose in it breast-side-up. Bake, covered, until meat begins to split away from breastbone—from 2 to 4 hours depending on size of bird. Baste every 30 minutes. The remaining wild rice can be served, moistened if necessary with broth or water, as a side dish. A bright-flavored fruit dish, such as cranberry sauce or cinnamon applesauce, adds sweetness to this rich and delicious meal.

WILD RICE–GOOSE CASSEROLE

This is a great way to use up already-cooked goose, and can be made with leftovers from Wild Rice Goose. Wild rice and goose are powerful flavors, especially together. Sour cream helps mellow and blend them. And it goes nicely with mushrooms.

1 onion, chopped
1 carrot, cubed
1 cup portabella or other mushrooms
1 garlic clove, chopped
Salt and pepper to taste
¼ teaspoon thyme
3 tablespoons butter
3 tablespoons flour
2 cups cooked wild rice
1 quart beef broth, heated
3 cups cooked goose or mallard, chopped
1 cup sour cream

Preheat oven to 300 degrees. Melt butter in Dutch oven or casserole that can go from the stovetop to the oven. Brown onion, carrot, garlic, and mushrooms. Add salt, pepper, and thyme. When onion is translucent, add flour and cook until lightly browned. Add beef broth and stir until flour is dissolved. Add goose. Bake covered for 1 hour. Remove from oven and uncover. When casserole stops bubbling, stir in sour cream. Serve over egg noodles or with sour-dough bread.

Wild Rice

Perhaps no other food is as strongly associated with a place as is wild rice (*Zizania palustris*) with the Upper Midwest. Indeed, the largest concentrations of this fascinating aquatic plant are found among the lakes and rivers of Michigan, Wisconsin, Minnesota, and southern Canada. But just as it's hard to find one's way paddling through dense stands of wild rice, it's difficult to know where to begin talking about wild rice

We'll start with history—the vital role it played for the early Native people of the Upper Midwest. The Ojibwe word *manoomin* means "the good berry" and also carries with it a deeper spiritual significance as a gift from the Great Spirit. A foundational Ojibwe belief is that they would know the right place to settle when they arrived at a place where food was growing on the water. This was, of course, the wild rice-rich country of what is now the northern United States and southern Canada—their traditional homeland. Bands, tribes, and communities came to depend on particular rice beds, just as European families depended on their family farms. No discussion of wild rice in the Upper Midwest is complete without mentioning the construction of the Chippewa Flowage by Minnesota Power and Light in 1924. While MPL promised to leave intact or restore thousands of acres of rice beds that belonged to the Lac Courte Oreilles band of Ojibwe, they did not honor this commitment. The effect of this on the LCO Ojibwe was profound, and has not been forgotten.

Despite the sometimes-sad history associated with this plant it is still a real force today in the Upper Midwest. Native and white, male and female, old and young, teams of ricers can still be seen in early autumn participating in this ancient harvest. In fact, the Ojibwe word for the late-August full moon is "ricing moon." One person poles a canoe or low-draft boat and another sits in the bow and strokes the tall rice canes with sticks called rice sticks. The ripe grass kernels—wild rice is actually a grass and not a member of the rice family—fall into the bottom of the boat. Once harvested, the rice is dried and then roasted.

In recent decades, commercial operations in California and Minnesota have begun to cultivate wild rice in large paddies and harvest it mechanically. This is the wild rice commonly found in large grocery stores. Truly wild—that is, uncultivated—wild rice can still be purchased at mom and pop outlets in the Northwoods, from tribal businesses, and at natural food stores. This uncultivated wild rice grows in the shallow inland lakes of the Great Lakes region. It is lighter in color, cooks more quickly, and commands a much higher price because of the extensive labor required to harvest and process it. Cultivated wild rice is more affordable and still a great accompaniment to game dishes. Its flavor and texture, however, are no match for the real item growing in nature.

Because it keeps so well, wild rice was an ideal, portable food for early Native people. It could be boiled into a soup or stew, or pounded into a flour and made into cakes. Today, the culinary uses of wild rice are even more diverse. The most common cooking method is simply simmering it in salted broth. Domestic or game meats—grouse, waterfowl, venison—can be added to this broth, as can carrots, celery, onions, and mushrooms. If a wild duck dinner is served in Wisconsin or Minnesota, chances are good that a dish of wild rice is also on the table. Waterfowl stuffed with cooked wild rice is another traditional recipe—and the signature dish of this cookbook! "Wild Rice" is the name of a restaurant in Bayfield, Wisconsin. It is also a staple item on many Upper Midwest menus, such as that of the Angry Trout Café in Grand Marais, Minnesota.

A handful of it added to a soup of wild turkey adds a special richness—at once nutty and earthy. It can also be baked, in casserole, with bratwurst and onions and sour cream. Or added to a meatloaf with some wild mushrooms. Or served in a cold salad with cranberries. And while we are speaking of things sweet, wild rice pancakes are a regional treat not to be missed. Drench them in local maple syrup and you will really taste the Upper Midwest!

But it's not just man that benefits from wild rice. It also plays an important role in the lifecycle of marshes. It is one of many wetland plants that act as filters for pollutants and sediment, thus improving water quality further downstream. The dense stands made by rice canes provide nesting and loafing cover for waterfowl, furbearers, and fish. Perhaps most important, wild rice seeds provide high-nutrient food for waterfowl before they make the long journey south. So strong is their affinity for this food that it's not uncommon to flush scores, even hundreds, of ducks from a single rice patch.

Staple food of Native people, link in the chain of an ecosystem, culinary inspiration—wild rice is a regional food in the truest sense of the word.

GRILLED GOOSE BREASTS

The meat of wild goose has a unique taste—at once red and iron-rich like beef but with the texture of poultry. Because wild goose can be dry, marinating and then grilling it is a good option. This also works well for large ducks like mallards. Goose or duck legs can be reserved for another use, such as soup. While this recipe uses red wine, other high-acid liquids—soy sauce, Worcestershire sauce, and orange juice, for example—also work well.

Breasts of 1 wild goose or 2 wild ducks
Salt and pepper to taste

Marinade
1 cup dry red wine
1 teaspoon herbes de Provence
1 garlic clove, minced
¼ cup olive oil
¼ teaspoon black pepper
½ teaspoon salt

Whisk together marinade ingredients. Lightly salt and pepper goose. Set in non-reactive container and cover with marinade. Refrigerate for as little as 4 hours or as long as 24 hours. Heat charcoal to ash-white or preheat gas grill. Remove goose from marinade and let drain. Grill goose breasts 5 minutes per side or until medium-rare. Be careful not to overcook. Slice across the grain and serve with robust red wine, homemade cranberry sauce, and garlic mashed potatoes.

GOOSE TOURTIERE

The hearty *tourtiere*, or French Canadian meat pie, evokes seventeenth-century Canada. Tasting its old-fashioned spices—cloves, allspice, and cinnamon—tucked inside a flaky crust, you can almost see a hungry voyageur sitting down to this, along with a cask of ale, as snow falls outside on the stone walls of the fort. Today, this dish is traditionally made with pork. But adding goose (or any game meat) is no stretch, since it was more abundant than domestic meat in the days of early settlement.

1 pound ground pork
1 pound or more ground goose (or any other ground game meat)
1 rutabaga, diced
1 large onion, diced
¾ teaspoon salt
½ teaspoon black pepper
½ teaspoon ground cinnamon
¼ teaspoon cloves
1 pinch ground allspice
½ cup water or flat beer
Butter, lard, or shortening for greasing baking dish
2 9-inch pie crusts (store-bought or home-made)
1 egg, beaten

Preheat oven to 350 degrees. Grease 9-inch baking dish. Brown pork and goose in skillet and add onion and rutabaga when fat starts to appear in pan; add spices and water or beer. Cook until rutabaga is soft and meat fully browned (about ½ hour). Line baking dish with bottom crust. Spoon meat-vegetable mixture onto crust. Cover with top crust. Crimp the edges with a fork and cut vents into the pie. Bake for 1 hour or until crust is brown, brushing periodically with egg.

Apricot Roasted Goose

Here the smoky-sweet taste of apricot plays off the dark, rich taste of goose. Bacon strips placed across the goose breast keep the bird moist. This is a festive dish, and really crowns the table for Thanksgiving, Christmas, or the New Year.

1 Canada, snow, or whitefront goose, plucked
Salt, pepper, and poultry seasoning to taste
1 quart of stale, cubed white bread (or equivalent
  in dry stuffing such as Brownberry)
2 tablespoons butter
1 onion, minced
1 cup dried apricots
2 cups orange juice
6 slices of thick bacon

Preheat oven to 300 degrees. Generously season goose inside and out with salt and pepper and poultry seasoning. Melt butter in skillet and cook onions until soft; mix cooked onion with apricots and bread cubes and loosely stuff goose. Now, pin bacon slices over the breast of the goose with toothpicks. Pour orange juice into the bottom of a large roasting pan, add goose to pan, breast-side-up. Bake, covered, until meat begins to split away from breastbone—from 2 to 4 hours depending on size of bird. Baste every 30 minutes with pan juices.

Early Season Goose

With local Canada geese being so abundant in the last few decades, natural resource departments across the Upper Midwest have responded by opening a season targeted at these big birds. The idea is to help control populations of an animal that has, in some places, become too numerous and at the same time to provide expanded opportunities for hunters. The season begins September 1 and runs about two weeks. Some traditionalists don't care for hunting in warm—often downright hot—weather. But I enjoy the generous bag limits and the chance to add a few weeks to the season. What's more, these birds are often well fed and tender because they have not migrated. Another thing to recommend for an early goose season is the abundance of local produce available. This recipe is very similar to the beloved Eastern European paprikás, where tomatoes and peppers—in a sour cream sauce—enhance the flavor of the meat.

> 1 Canada goose, skinned and cut into serving-size pieces
> Salt, pepper, and paprika to taste
> Flour for dredging
> 4 tablespoons olive oil or lard
> 1 large onion, diced
> 1 green bell pepper or 2 banana or wax peppers, cored,
>   seeded and chopped
> 4 ripe tomatoes, cored and chopped
> 1 quart chicken broth, hot
> 1 cup sour cream

Season goose pieces generously with salt, pepper, and paprika. Dredge in flour. Brown in the bottom of a heavy kettle in oil or lard. Remove goose to a warm platter and cook onions in the same kettle until clear; add pepper, tomatoes, and broth. Replace goose pieces and cook until tender—1½ to 2 hours. Remove bones, turn off heat, and stir in sour cream to thicken. You can also make this in a crockpot by first browning the meat and onions in a skillet and transferring them—along with the tomatoes, peppers, and broth—to the crockpot and cooking on low for 4 to 6 hours. Remove bones and thicken as described for stovetop recipe. Serve over egg noodles or mashed potatoes.

Roast Goose with Sauerkraut

A nod to Upper Midwest immigrants from Germany and Eastern Europe, this dish is festive and hearty. The sharpness of sauerkraut contrasts nicely with the dark, rich goose. It also helps tenderize the meat. A crisp lager beer, homemade applesauce, oven-browned potatoes, and black bread make this a memorable meal.

1 Canada, snow, or whitefront goose, plucked
Salt and pepper to taste
1 teaspoon Hungarian paprika (sweet or hot)
1 onion, sliced
1 apple with skin on, sliced
8 slices of bacon—4 coarsely chopped, 4 left whole
1 quart jarred sauerkraut, drained

Preheat oven to 300 degrees. Generously season goose inside and out with salt and pepper and paprika. Cook the coarse-chopped bacon in skillet until it is almost brown; do not drain. Brown onion and apple in drippings and toss with sauerkraut, leaving in the browned bacon pieces. Stuff goose loosely with kraut mixture. If there is leftover kraut, place it—with the wine—in the bottom of the roaster in which you plan to cook the goose. Now, pin the remaining bacon strips onto the goose breast with toothpicks. Baste every 30 minutes and cook until meat begins to split from breastbone—usually 2 to 4 hours depending on the size of the bird. This gentle "splitting" is a sign that the bird is tender and done. When bird is done, allow to rest for ½ hour. Place kraut stuffing in center of platter and surround with carved goose. For a rich gravy, skim off the fat from pan drippings, simmer, and thicken with flour.

Coot in Gravy

Coot are the undeserved butt of many a duck blind joke, because they are less wary than wild ducks and, supposedly, poor table fare. The joke, however, may be on the joke-makers, since coot can be fine eating if handled properly. They also provide good sport if the ducks aren't flying. I've spent many a slow afternoon paddling my skiff through lotus or wild rice beds jumping them up and shooting them on the wing as I would with a wood duck or teal. The trick with preparing coot for the table is trimming off all fat, which holds a strong taste, and keeping them moist as they cook.

> Breasts and legs of 2 coot, trimmed of any fat/skin
>   and soaked in salt water for 1 hour
> Flour seasoned heavily with salt and pepper
> 4 tablespoons bacon fat or butter
> 2 cups chicken broth, hot
> 1 large onion, sliced
> 1 cup button mushrooms, sliced
> 1 handful of flat leaf parsley, chopped
> Salt and pepper to taste

Dredge coot pieces in seasoned flour. Brown in bacon fat or butter in large, deep skillet. When golden on both sides, add onion, mushrooms, and parsley to the pan. Be careful the onion doesn't burn. Add broth and cook until coot is tender, about 1½ hours. If stew is not thick enough for your liking, remove 1 cup of cooking liquid and whisk in 4 tablespoons of flour and ¼ cup of milk. Return this to the hot pan and cook only until stew thickens. Serve with wild rice or mashed potatoes.

FISH

It's a daunting task to cast a net around all the fishing venues in the Upper Midwest. For starters, the combined total of inland lakes in Michigan, Wisconsin, and Minnesota numbers just under 40,000. Yup, that's 40,000—no typo. Add to this large chunks of real estate on sprawling Great Lakes Huron, Michigan, and Superior and this kettle of fish becomes bigger still. Then, of course, there are thousands of flowing waters, great—like the Mississippi and Missouri—and small— from Northwoods rivulets to gentle farm-country meanders.

The list of species is as grand and varied as the places to fish. Coldwater quarry include brook trout, rainbow trout, brown trout, lake trout, whitefish, and salmon. And coolwater / warmwater fish? You'll find the full complement: muskellunge and northern pike, walleye and smallmouth bass, largemouth bass and panfish, catfish and rough fish, plus a few oddballs like smelt and sturgeon. Clearly, no short essay can do justice to the Upper Midwest's vast universe of fisheries. It took six hundred pages in my *Fly Fisher's Guide to Wisconsin and Iowa* to cover just two states! Still, *something* needs to be said about the fish themselves, the places where they live, and how to clean them.

MANY RIVERS TO FISH—AND SOME GREAT LAKES

Fisheries regions across the Upper Midwest might be described as Great Lakes, Northwoods, and farm country. Great Lakes fishing can take place on the lakes themselves—from a boat or from shore—and in the tributaries that feed them; it centers around trout and salmon. Anyone looking to fish the open waters of the Great Lakes is best served by finding a friend or trusty charter captain with dependable boat. These inland seas are nothing to trifle with, and trolling multiple lines at various depths is best left to experts. Shore-fishing trout and salmon anglers target harbors, river mouths, breakwaters, and warm-water-discharging power plants where baitfish gather. From Minnesota's North Shore on Lake Superior to the Lake Michigan breakwaters near Milwaukee, a cut smelt is the favored bait; salmon eggs and spoons are also popular. Great Lakes rivers known for trout and salmon runs include Michigan's Pere Marquette (near Ludington), Big Two Hearted, and St. Mary's (in the eastern Upper Peninsula); Wisconsin's Bois Brule (west of Bayfield), Oconto (flowing into Green Bay's west shore), and Ahnapee (in southern Door County); Minnesota's Lester and French (near Duluth) and Temperance (near Grand Marais). Bright streamers, egg flies, and big nymphs are go-to fly patterns; small lures and eggs sacks are popular with spin fishers. Coolwater species like smallmouth bass, northern pike, walleye, and perch frequent bays, harbors, and the lower ends of tributary rivers. They are pursued using the usual methods like minnows, spoons, or jigs. These warmer, shallow areas—like Huron's Lake St. Clair, Wisconsin's Green Bay, and Superior's Chequamegon Bay—are also popular ice fishing destinations.

A handy starting point for talking about Northwoods fisheries is the 45th parallel, which marks the southern boundary of Northwoods fisheries across these three states. Follow it from the south shore of Michigan's Upper Peninsula, westward through Wisconsin, and into Minnesota; in Minnesota, follow a line north of Interstate 94 to the Canadian border. Look at all those lakes—tens of thousands of them! Only Ontario and Finland have a higher density of lakes. These forested lakes and the rivers that run among them have a distinctly northern feel, cloaked in forests of pine, aspen, maple, and birch. Fire up the old outboard and putter along likely cover. Hit fallen trees for largemouth bass, lily pad bays for northern pike and panfish, and rocky drop-off for smallmouth and walleye. What to put on the end of your line? Nightcrawlers—fished beneath a float or with a weight—catch a lot of fish, as do minnows and leeches. Red and white spoons of the Daredevle type are tops for pike, surface plugs are go-to for largemouths, and deep-running crankbaits will take smallmouth and walleye. An east-to-west list of standout Northwoods lakes would have to include Lake Gogebic in the western Upper Peninsula of Michigan, the Menominee Flowage on the Wisconsin-Michigan line, the many wilderness lakes of Wisconsin's Northern American Highlands American Legion State Forest, the waters great and small of Minnesota's Boundary Waters, and sprawling Lake of the Woods on the Minnesota-Canada border. At this northern latitude, with prolonged winters, most streams and rivers are coldwater trout fisheries. The Au Sable, Manistee, Fox, and Ontanogan top the list for Michigan. The Wolf, Prairie, and Brule are Wisconsin's crown jewels, with Minnesota's finest feeding into Lake Superior occurring near Grand Marais. Fly anglers prospect with streamers and nymphs, or fish to hatches. Spinning anglers use worms, minnows, and small lures.

Southern lower Michigan, southern Wisconsin, southern Minnesota, and Iowa are in a region that might be called farm country. Lakes are scarce and mostly manmade. (Lake Winnebago, Wisconsin's largest inland lake at nearly 130,000 acres, is naturally occurring and an important exception.) Farm-country rivers host a mix of bass, catfish, walleye, and northern pike. The largest river systems are the Mississippi, Missouri, Red, Wisconsin, Iowa, and Minnesota. The network of smaller rivers is vast indeed. These are the sorts of places where a couple of guys might float the hidden stretches between bridges in an old jon boat on a Sunday afternoon. Michigan's Grand and St. Joseph, Wisconsin's Chippewa and Black, Iowa's Turkey and Wapsipinicon, Minnesota's Otter Tail and Crow Wing—even the names evoke a quiet poetry of summer evenings and owl calls. They may not yield state record fish or draw big crowds. But for the anglers who fish them, they are home waters.

Within farm country, the small triangle-shaped piece of land known as the unglaciated or Driftless area—mainly in Wisconsin but with a swatch in northeast Iowa and southeast Minnesota—hosts productive, spring-fed trout streams. These small streams rarely freeze up in winter; there's a constant supply of forage like scuds, minnows, and crawfish. This combination makes for some first-rate trout fishing. Standouts here are the Timber Coulee system near Coon Valley, Wisconsin; Waterloo Creek in northeast Iowa; and Hay Creek near Red Wing, Minnesota.

Think Like a Fish: Find Food and Shelter

Trout streams seem as good a place to begin as any, because trout streams are microcosms of larger waters. Imagine it's opening day and you are on the stream after a winter of ice fishing, or just sitting around and putting on a few pounds, which can be raised to an art form with all the great beer and cheese and sausage around. You notice there's a lot of water but it's not all the same. Here it slips under the bank; there it curls up against a tree. Way downstream, it plunges into a deep hole. And perhaps upstream, by that big dead elm where you stuffed your shirt pockets with morels last opening day, it goes flat—deep and lagoon-like. When the winter mind has dissipated, you begin to think like a fish. Or like any animal. Where would I go to get a maximum of food with a minimum of effort?

You find yourself zeroing in on places where a fish can eat and find protection. So, you snake a streamer beneath the fallen tree below you, twitching it, and WHAM. There goes the purple-blue form twisting in the water and you are working him back toward you, into the net. You dispatch him on a rock and gut him and then wrap him in the burlap basmati rice bag where he'll stay cool and fresh. One down, two to go. And then maybe you'll check that elm for mushrooms. Or hit the tavern on the way home for breakfast. Or maybe check the ditch on West River Road to see if those first asparagus spears are up yet. But, you're ahead of yourself. You're only one third of the way there. Trout number two comes from the deep, open pool above you—a gimme fish. You drifted a nymph and he smacked it. But try that pool later in the day, when the sun is on it and you can see to the bottom, you will get nary a strike. Food might be there, but with sunlight on the pool, shelter is gone. No equation, no fish.

While you're upstream, you decide to continue in that direction. There had always been a deep hole against a limestone boulder here—and usually a good fish or two. But when you round the bend, you see the hole is gone. It's silted up from spring rains. There's a part of you that feels cheated. "I was counting on this," you say. But, after a breath or two, you realize it doesn't work this way. Nothing is permanent but change. The Lord giveth and taketh away. Choose your phrase. The point is, streams are always changing, and so anglers, to be successful, must adapt.

In your newfound clarity, you see some fresh growth on the far bank—a bunch of blackberry bushes. The water sweeps against them, disappears into a sort of grotto, and you watch. There's a small rise. And then a larger rise. You change to an Adams dry fly, nice and bushy. The first cast is short. Then you get it right in the eddy. You're watching it float by and then, all of a sudden, it disappears. Game on! This is a good fish. And you can see from the burnt-almond color that it's a brown. You turn him with your rod into the open water and pretty much have him beat.

This is a bit longwinded, perhaps. But it's how I learned to fish—on small waters with wary trout. As I graduated to big water—reedy northern lakes or sprawling rivers like the Mississippi—I employed lessons learned on small streams. A friend of mine has a lake cottage way up in Wisconsin's Vilas County. In years passed, we had managed to catch a few—but not enough for a proper fish fry or to justify getting up at 5 AM—in a channel that had some weeds and sand humps. We'd gotten information at a tavern—try on the other side of the boathouse—but it was pretty vague. We anchored over some weeds and fished, anchored and fished. But it was only when we found a hole *in* the weeds that we really got onto them. Big, humpbacked perch and dark, dinner-plate-sized bluegill. The reason? We were fishing right on top of their habitat. The weeds gave them shelter and the little bugs and minnows living in them gave them food.

I've used the same lesson in Badger state waters like the Black, Wisconsin, and Mississippi; Hawkeye waters like the Turkey and Yellow; and bigger rivers and flowages in Michigan like Bay De Noc and the Ausable, Fox, Two Hearted, and Menominee as well as countless reedy little lakes. Another trip that comes to mind is a camping trip to the Menominee with my friend Mike Egle. While our wives readied the coals in anticipation of fresh fish, we shoved off in Mike's trusty V-hull. I hung back and let Mike select the spots—and was immensely relieved to find that I was in the company of another structure guy. Lots of boats were anchored in the channel, randomly fishing for walleye. We buzzed around rocky drop-offs, points, and lily pad bays and came back with a mixed bag of northern pike, smallmouth bass, and walleye. The reason for our success? Mike fished the big flowage like a giant trout stream. Unless there's a heavy-duty hatch on, you don't just fish the main stream. You look for rocks, overhangs, shaded holes. And so we looked for points, boulders, lily pads—and cleaned up. In my float trips down Upper Midwest rivers, I've used the "trout stream" approach with equally good results. Deadfalls are a great place to fish. Another favorite of mine are the ubiquitous springs that feed these rivers, especially in summer. They are northern pike magnets. At times, they also attract some very large brown trout as well as walleye, smallmouth, channel catfish, and panfish.

While fishing on the open waters of the Great Lakes themselves requires special equipment and special techniques—chief among them a seaworthy boat and dependable motor—I believe the trout stream approach can be applied to Great Lakes shoreline and tributaries. Steelhead and Great Lakes run trout return to the streams where they were released as fingerlings. They are not actively feeding but spawning where conditions permit—as in a handful of Lake Superior tributaries like the Brule—and attempting to spawn in other waters. This is important to keep in mind because you are trying to entice them, rather than simulating prey species. Look for these lake-run fish in the same sorts of places you find regular stream trout—resting places like current breaks, deadfalls, or overhanging banks. Waterfalls and dams are natural barriers and can gather large numbers of fish in season. Egg sacks, flies, and spinners are all popular methods. Fish in the harbors may be feeding more actively, so dead smelt and spoons are popular in these waters.

So-called rough fish can make for good sport and eating with certain important caveats. That is, they tend to be best if taken from cold, clear water. And in the case of sheepshead, they are best to eat—in my experience—from swift-flowing rivers. The sheepshead I've eaten from lakes throughout the region have a softer flesh and a strong taste. Taken from waters like the Mississippi, Upper Iowa, and Kickapoo Rivers, however, they have been well worth eating, with a taste and texture similar to crappie. Like crappie, they need to be kept on ice. And fillet out the mud vein on both species. Similarly, any sucker or redhorse you catch in a trout stream will be firm and sweet. The large number of bones, however, makes pickling the only viable cooking option. The bones dissolve—and succulent chunks of meat remain, that go well on a Ritz cracker chased down by a cold beer. A little dill never hurts, either. Diminutive smelt are caught in dip nets, in Great Lakes tributaries, right around ice-out. Look for figures on the beach warming themselves around trash-can fires.

IN THE PAN

While the universe of species to fish and venues in which to fish them is broad across the Upper Midwest, some basic truths hold for care and cooking of all fish. First, put fish on ice as soon as is practical after catching them. This might be an ice chest full of cubes or blocks, or a refrigerator if you're fishing close to home. The only time when this is not an issue is ice fishing, where you have plenty of ready-made ice at hand. Now, some anglers keep their quarry alive in livewells or wire baskets kept in the water. If the water is cold, this is fine. But in still water, during midsummer, I don't recommend it. Some species like catfish and northern pike stay alive and intact. Others, however, such as crappie and bass, begin to get mushy. The simplest solution is a cooler. If you're fishing along a trout stream, a cooler is hard to carry. I slip a small burlap bag in my fishing vest. I gut each fish after catching it and keep the gutted fish in the burlap bag, where it will be cool and fresh. Wicker creels accomplish the same thing but are harder to manage along a brushy stream. Canvas creels work well, if you can find one. Canvas field bags sold at army surplus stores will also work. But you get the principle: keep your fish cool and out of the sun.

Whether to gut, steak, or fillet depends on the fish and your preference. Gutting is a good approach for smaller fish. I recommend it for small trout, small panfish, bullheads, and smaller channel catfish. Many fish cooks, myself included, feel keeping the head on adds flavor. Others don't care for this as it might put off diners. Gutted panfish—or any fish other than trout and catfish—need to be scaled after gutting. Once the fish is gutted, you can choose whether to fry it up and let folks eat right to the bone, or to simmer it for a soup or fish cakes—in which case the meat is stripped off the bone once it's cooked and the liquid saved for making a sauce or broth. An exception to the gut-the-small-fish rule is large fish that will be baked whole.

For stronger-tasting fish, like catfish, carp, and sheepshead, you must remove all the fat before cooking them. This fat is found between the skin and the "meat" of the fillet. In carp and sheepshead, this fat shows up as a red-brown line running more or less parallel to the spine. In catfish and bullheads, this is often yellow in color and located in the same place; some catfish have it on their bellies as well. Trim this off, even if it means sacrificing meat.

Fish will last two or three days on ice or in the refrigerator. Promptly freeze any fish you do not plan to eat right away. And get all the air out the packages before you freeze them. A vacuum sealer is one way to accomplish this. Another way is to store them in ziplock bags. Fish keeps reasonably well in the freezer for up to six months. After that, it becomes freezer-burnt and loses its flavor or develops off flavors. So, ice it down, eat it right away, or freeze it tight. Do that, and you'll be assured fine eating—and a lot of fun in the process.

TROUT CAKES

This is an excellent way to introduce first-timers to trout. There are no bones to deal with and the seasoned cakes, cooked in butter, are very sweet, almost like crab. There are almost innumerable flavor variations for trout cakes. For a Latin taste, add lime and cumin instead of lemon and Old Bay and substitute corn tortillas for breadcrumbs. Dill, green onions, or any other herb can be used in place of Old Bay.

3 small (or 1 very large) trout, gutted
1 egg, beaten
1 cup of breadcrumbs or stale grated French bread
2 tablespoons mayonnaise
1 tablespoon lemon juice
1 teaspoon Old Bay or fish seasoning of choice
3 tablespoons butter for browning

Sauce
1 tablespoon butter
1 tablespoon flour
1 tablespoon lemon juice
1 cup of liquid used to cook fish, strained

Slowly simmer trout in water until fish begins to flake from the bone—about 20 minutes. Remove fish from broth; cool and debone. Add beaten egg, breadcrumbs, mayonnaise, and lemon juice. Mix all together and form into patties. Season patties, on both sides, with Old Bay or fish seasoning. Brown cakes on both sides, in butter, and serve hot. A simple sauce can be made from the broth. Strain and reserve 1 cup of it; keep hot. In a small saucepan, melt 1 tablespoon butter and quickly blend in 1 tablespoon flour. Add hot broth and stir until smooth. Add 1 tablespoon lemon juice, correct seasoning with salt and pepper, and serve over cakes.

POACHED TROUT WITH LEMON SAUCE

Large trout take well to poaching, as do trout or salmon steaks and fillets. No, this isn't bland nursing home food! It's a change from the usual pan frying or grilling—and elegant when served with a light lemon sauce.

1 whole 2-pound trout, gutted, or equivalent in salmon steaks or fillets
Salt and pepper to taste
Half of 1 lemon
Fresh dill sprigs
1 quart fish stock

Sauce
1 tablespoon butter
1 tablespoon flour
1 tablespoon lemon juice
1 cup of liquid used to cook fish, strained

Preheat oven to warm. In a kettle large enough to fit fish, bring fish stock to a low boil; add dill. Season fish with salt and pepper and rub with cut lemon. Place fish in stock and cook until translucent, until fish just begins to flake. Leave stock warm on stovetop. Remove fish to a platter and keep in a warm oven while making the lemon sauce. To make the lemon sauce, begin by straining and reserving 1 cup of stock. In a small saucepan, melt 1 tablespoon butter and quickly blend in 1 tablespoon flour. Add hot broth and stir until smooth. Add 1 tablespoon lemon juice, correct seasoning with salt and pepper, and serve over fish. Asparagus, brown or wild rice, and white wine will round out the meal nicely.

TROUT WITH HAM

This is an American take on a Spanish classic. In Spain, trout is cooked until crispy in olive oil—with a slice of air-cured ham, jamón Serrano, added at the very end. Jamón Serrano, however, can be difficult to find outside of major cities and is too salty for many American palates. *Do* spend the money on Virginia or other good-quality ham, though, as the water-added product doesn't hold up. Also, use small or medium-size trout, the fresher the better. I leave the head on because it adds flavor. If you find this off-putting, feel free to remove it.

> **Any number of trout (8 to 12 inches long), gutted, with heads left on**
> **Salt and pepper to taste**
> **1 lemon, cut into wedges**
> **Small handful of flour**
> **Good-quality, air-cured ham, 1 slice per fish**
> **1 tablespoon peanut oil for each trout**

Clean the cavity of each trout well. You can use your fingernail or a very small knife to remove any blood or other matter. Quickly rinse each fish in cold running water. This can also be done right at the stream or lake. For each fish, take a lemon wedge and squeeze it all over the trout, inside and out; season each fish with salt and pepper. Then, dust with flour. Heat a skillet (or skillets) of sufficient size to cook the fish without crowding. Bear in mind, you'll also be adding a ham slice for each trout. Heat oil. Cook fish until brown—4 to 5 minutes per side. During last minute of cooking, add ham slice to skillet and cook until crisp. Serve fish, one per diner, wrapped in or next to ham slice with a wedge of lemon on the side. Cornbread, baked beans, and cold beer make good accompaniments, as do oven-browned potatoes with thyme.

SALMON WITH CHIMICHURRI

Sharp, pesto-like chimichurri works well with bold flavors. It's a nice change from the more familiar ways of cooking salmon. A friendly word of warning: chimichurri is highly addictive. You'll soon be spreading it on steak, chicken, French bread, fresh vegetables, and just about anything else that's edible.

1 pound salmon steaks of fillets
1 tablespoon olive oil

Chimichurri
½ cup Italian parsley
½ cup cilantro
½ cup olive oil
2 garlic cloves, minced
⅓ cup red wine vinegar
½ teaspoon cumin
½ teaspoon salt
Pinch of sugar

Place all ingredients for chimichurri in food processor and chop until a smooth paste is formed; let this stand for 30 minutes in the refrigerator. Preheat gas grill or have coals ashed-over and ready to cook. Lightly coat each side of salmon pieces with olive oil, then cover with chimichurri. Cook 5 minutes on each side. Serve with roasted potatoes, fruit or green salad, and a chilled rosé wine.

Grilled Whitefish

This relative of the trout and grayling thrives in cold, clear waters above the 45th parallel. If you had to pick one fish associated with the northern Great Lakes, whitefish would be it. They're the mainstay of commercial fishermen on Lakes Michigan and Superior, and a favorite of sport anglers as well. For centuries, they have also been a staple—both fresh and dried—of Native people living in the Upper Midwest. You'll find them for sale in fish shops of Great Lakes harbors. You'll also sometimes find them in the seafood case of grocery stores further south. Whitefish has firm, sweet flesh and is equally delicious smoked, in a fish boil, pickled with dill and onions, or grilled, as in this recipe.

    1 pound whitefish fillets·
    ½ teaspoon herb seasoning, such as Penzey's Fox Point,
       or more to taste
    Salt and pepper to taste
    1 lemon, cut into wedges
    2 tablespoons melted butter

Preheat gas grill or have charcoal ashed-over and glowing. Season fillets with herb seasoning and salt and pepper. Squeeze fresh lemon juice over fillets, then melted butter. Place fillets on buttered aluminum foil or fish grate. Cook until fish just begins to flake—about 10 minutes. Serve with boiled potatoes and chilled white wine.

A Tough, Cold, Rewarding Job

Up before dawn in all kinds of weather—watching tip-ups when it's ten below, fishing walleye during spring floods, braving mosquito-thick backwaters—sport fishermen consider themselves a pretty rugged lot. Compared to the general run of people, sport fishermen are pretty rugged. But how rugged is rugged? Do they drive their boats through thick ice for a mile just to get out fishing? Use chainsaws to clear a frozen river channel? Fish on the Great Lakes during high seas? Wrestle with angry snapping turtles? Operate heavy machinery that could pull them into frigid waters? This is no extreme sport or reality TV show. And there aren't very many people up to the task. But a few hearty souls still make their living by dropping nets into the Great Lakes and Mississippi River—hoping Mother Nature and the price of fish will treat them well.

For the Native people living in the region and for early European settlers, the Great Lakes and large rivers of the Upper Midwest seemed to provide an unlimited bounty of whitefish, lake trout, and yellow perch. Populations of these fish held steady, for the most part, into the early twentieth century. However, untreated sewage discharged from Great Lakes ports began to pollute the waters. The arrival of alien species—such as sea lampreys, alewifes, and later zebra mussels—and overfishing also took their further toll. Now, Lake Michigan stocks of whitefish and perch are only a fraction of what they were; commercial lake trout fishing is now closed. Colder, cleaner Lake Superior still has a stable whitefish population, but its diminished lake trout population permits only a small commercial harvest. While the Upper Mississippi River has decent numbers of the rough fish sought by commercial fishermen, getting to them—and selling the fish for a decent price—is not an easy matter. "It's not a job for unstable people," says fifth-generation commercial fisherman Mike Valley, who runs Valley Fish and Cheese in Prairie du Chien, Wisconsin.

In principle, commercial fishing in the Upper Midwest is pretty simple. Fishermen set their nets in likely places and return later to check them. The reality of this work, however, is a lot tougher. To begin with, just returning to your nets in winter can be difficult. Great Lakes boats must break through ice for up to a mile just to get out of the harbor. Then, once they've reached their nets, ice has formed in them and retrieval becomes a challenge. Mississippi River fisherman clear ice using chainsaws and augers and bring in their nets by hand. (Imagine hauling hundreds of pounds of fish and ice while standing in a rocking boat on a sub-zero morning!) Also, during storms or high winds, nets (and the fish in them) can be carried away—with thousands of dollars in product and gear lost. Fish caught in the nets must be sorted by hand, with only legal species kept. Gamefish and other unpermitted species have to be released. The catch must be kept fresh and cold while being transported back to the shop, where it is sold and processed. Even the best commercial fishermen experience slumps. And then there is the upkeep for boats and nets.

Still, there's satisfaction to be had in being your own boss, and doing what you love. Says Mike Valley about fishing on the Upper Mississippi, "When it's going good and things are clicking along—this a great place to be."

"I've tried other things, but I miss the fishing," says Chris Peterson, captain of Peterson Fisheries in Hancock, in Michigan's Upper Peninsula. "I love the hunt." Peterson is one of a few dozen commercial fishermen still working on Lake Superior. Peterson credits his success in part to milder winters, which allow him more time on the water. Peterson fishes nearly every day of the year—except for Christmas, Thanksgiving, and when the seas are over eight feet. Peterson's family operates Four Sons Fish and Chips and Peterson's Fish Market.

You can learn more at museums like Roger's Street Fishing Village and Coast Guard Museum in Two Rivers, Wisconsin; the Great Lake Shipwreck Museum in Sault Ste. Marie, Michigan; the Lake Superior Maritime Museum in Duluth; and the Upper Mississippi River Museum and Aquarium in Dubuque. But you can also have a bite of history today—and support local food while you're at it. Want something really special for a holiday meal? Try whitefish caviar from Peterson's in Hancock, Michigan. Bored with bratwurst? How about whitefish sausage from Bearcat's Fish Market in Algoma, Wisconsin? Want a different kind of fish fry? Order fried herring at the Angry Trout Café in Grand Marais, Minnesota. Sick of the same old smoked salmon? Snag some smoked carp at Valley's Fish and Cheese in Prairie du Chien, Wisconsin. Don't feel like traveling? Pick up the phone or click the mouse. Whitefish that was swimming in Lake Superior yesterday could be at your door tomorrow. For a full listing of Upper Midwest fish markets specializing in local-caught fish, see the list of Wildfoods vendors at the back of this book.

Denny Weiss's Microwave Fish Fillets

Any recipe from Denny Weiss—an Iowa DNR employee and lifelong outdoorsman who gives wildfood cooking demonstrations at the state fair—comes highly recommended. What's more, this is healthy and requires very little cleanup. The trick is to make sure fillets are dry to begin with, then to drain off any cooking liquid. No one wants soggy fish!

1 pound panfish or walleye fillets, blotted dry with paper towels
½ teaspoon Old Bay or fish seasoning of choice, or more to taste
½ cup crushed Ritz crackers
½ cup grated cheddar cheese

Make sure fish fillets are patted dry. If not, continue to blot with paper towels. Season fish fillets to your liking. Place in casserole dish. Microwave fillets for 50 seconds; then drain off any liquid. Rotate fillets, so fillets that were in the center are on the edges and those on the edges are now in the center. Microwave for another 50 seconds and, again, drain off any liquid. Spread crushed crackers over fish and sprinkle cheese over crackers. Microwave until cheese is bubbling—about 30 seconds. *Note:* It may take some experimenting to get the cooking time right for your particular microwave.

Fried Smelt

Ask about smelting outside the Great Lakes states and people will think you're talking about melting metal. In these parts, however, it's the early spring event of dip-netting at Great Lakes river mouths to catch little silver fish. The smelt—sometimes pronounced *schmelt*—are then gutted with your fingernail, breaded, and fried in big kettles over garbage can fires or hauled home in gunnysacks and cooked there. Like ice fishing and deer hunting, smelting is one of those Upper Midwest cold-weather pursuits—smelt runs happen as the ice goes out in March and April. The secrets to cooking smelt are having the oil very hot, keeping the breading light, and making sure not to crowd the pan. Fried smelt should crunch as you bite down, almost like potato chips. Smelt can be purchased fresh, in spring, from Great Lakes fish shops or frozen year-round in the grocery store.

1 pound smelt, gutted (thaw frozen fish in refrigerator)
Fish breading mix, such as Shore Lunch or Fry Magic
Cooking oil

Tartar sauce
½ cup chopped pickles
1 cup mayonnaise

Bread smelt and shake off excess crumbs. Add oil to large kettle or fry pan to a depth of 1 inch; heat until bubbling. Drop smelt in a few at a time, making sure not to crowd pan. Too many fish in the pan cools the oil and makes the fish soggy. (A 10-inch skillet can handle 3 or 4 smelt at a time.) When first side is crisp, flip and cook until crisp on the other side. Drain on cookie sheets lined with newspaper or paper grocery bags. Once drained, smelt can be kept on a platter in a warm oven. For tartar sauce, mix chopped pickles with mayonnaise. Serve with lemon wedges and tartar sauce. Allow ⅓ to ½ pound of smelt per person.

Cathy Czachor's Bluegill

Fried bluegill fillets are my daughter's favorite food. And not just any bluegill, but bluegill fried by our friend Cathy Czachor. Cathy uses a Fry Daddy, but her fish cooking is more about technique than equipment. The fish are fresh, the breading light, the oil hot, and the number of fillets in each batch small. Fillets of small catfish—or whole bullheads, skinned and gutted—are also good in this recipe.

1 pound bluegill (or other panfish) fillets
Breading of choice: mix such as Shore Lunch or Fry Magic, bread crumbs,
    or ½ cup each of flour and cornmeal seasoned with salt and pepper
Cooking oil

As with fried smelt, this recipe calls for advance kitchen preparation. Line cookie sheets with paper bags or newspaper. Bread fish and shake off excess. Have oil hot and bubbling. You can use a specially designed fryer like a Fry Daddy, an electric skillet, or even a saucepan or iron skillet. Fill fryer with oil according to specific instructions or add oil to a depth of 1 inch in pan. Cook fillets a few at a time in hot oil, turning when one side is done and repeating on the other side. Remove fillets with slotted spoon; drain. Place drained fillets on platter in warmed oven. Serve with lemon wedges, coleslaw, and potato of choice.

Fish Tacos

As the population of Hispanic immigrants in the Midwest has grown over the past two decades, Latin grocery stores and restaurants have become fixtures of many small towns. Mainstays like steak tacos and beef burritos were immediate hits—with tamales, enchiladas, and tortas gaining currency after that. Fish tacos have taken a little longer to catch on. But once you try crunchy fish wrapped in a corn tortilla and smothered in creamy white sauce, you'll be hooked.

1 pound panfish fillets (bluegill, crappie, or perch) or fillets of larger fish
    (bass or walleye) cut into small pieces
Oil for frying
1 package corn tortillas
1 cup guacamole, or more as needed
½ cup fresh cilantro, chopped
1 cup green cabbage, shredded
1 lime, cut into wedges (optional)
1 cup pico de gallo, or more as needed (optional)
1 cup Monterey Jack cheese, shredded, or more as needed (optional)

Batter
1 cup beer
1 cup flour
2 tablespoons cornstarch
1 teaspoon baking powder
1 teaspoon salt
1 beaten egg

Cream sauce
1 cup mayonnaise
¼ cup parmesan cheese
1 teaspoon lime juice, or more to taste

Before frying the fish, have all the accompaniments ready—the batter whisked
together, the cream sauce mixed, the guacamole and pico de gallo in serving bowl, the cabbage
shredded, the cilantro chopped. Tortillas can be heated in a lightly oiled fry pan and kept
warm in a dishtowel. Heat oil in a deep skillet. Dip a few fish pieces at a time in batter; shake
off excess. Drop into skillet and cook until crisp; oil should be about ¼ of an inch deep. Drain
fried fish pieces and keep on platter in warm oven. Repeat until all pieces are cooked. The
"classic" fish taco contains a piece of fish, a dollop of cream sauce, a sprinkle of cilantro,
shredded cabbage, and a few spoonfuls of guacamole, all wrapped in a hot corn tortilla.
Shredded cheese, pico de gallo, and rice and beans are also good.

Fish Cakes

This recipe is very close to the recipe for trout cakes given earlier in the chapter. Here, however, we use leftover fish instead of fresh-cooked fish—and any leftover fish will work here, including saltwater species, smoked fish, baked fish, or poached fish.

2 cups leftover cooked fish, flaked and free of bones
1 egg, beaten
1 cup breadcrumbs or stale grated French bread
2 tablespoons mayonnaise
1 tablespoon lemon juice
1 teaspoon Old Bay or fish seasoning of choice
3 tablespoons butter for browning

Combine fish, beaten egg, breadcrumbs, mayonnaise, and lemon juice. Mix together and form into patties. Season patties, on both sides, with Old Bay or fish seasoning. Brown cakes on both sides, in butter, and serve hot. If you would like a sauce with your fish cakes, follow the instructions for making a lemon sauce given in the Trout Cakes recipe earlier in this chapter. Fish cakes can be served as a sandwich, main dish, or appetizer.

WALLEYE ALMONDINE

Delicate and sweet is the name of the game here—both the fish and nuts. Watch the heat and take care to crisp, not burn, the almonds.

1 pound walleye fillets; smallmouth bass taken from cold water
    may be substituted
Salt and pepper to taste
½ cup breadcrumbs
2 tablespoons butter and 2 tablespoons peanut oil,
    plus additional butter if necessary
½ cup chopped almonds
1 lemon, cut into wedges

Preheat oven to warm. Wipe fillets with a paper towel until dry, then season with salt and pepper. Dredge them in breadcrumbs, shaking off any excess. Heat oil and butter in large skillet. Brown fillets, a few at a time, making sure not to crowd the pan; keep in platter in warm oven. When all fish has been cooked, quickly sauté almonds in butter—adding more if pan is dry. Serve fish topped with almonds and browned butter and with a lemon wedge on the side. Coleslaw and rice pilaf are good sides for this special meal.

SMOKED CARP

I held a low opinion of eating carp until a few years ago. After a cold day ice fishing on the Upper Mississippi River, I stopped in at my friend Mike Valley's fish shop in Prairie du Chien, Wisconsin. He invited me out back to the smokehouse and set down a big slab of fish, which we both went to work on. The fish was delicious—firm and sweet with the tang of hickory wood. I was surprised to learn it was carp. But not just any carp. Mike targets smaller fish—in the two- to three-pound range—from very cold water. Brining also helps remove any disagreeable flavor.

1 carp (2- or 3-pounds), gutted, rinsed, and head removed
Brine made from 1½ cups salt and 1 gallon water
1 cup barbeque sauce for glaze (optional)

In a large food-grade metal, plastic, or stoneware container, soak carp in brine for 24 hours, then rinse well in cold running water. Pat dry. Place natural hardwood charcoal off to one side on the lower grate of your grill—start with a generous handful. When these are gray and ashed-over, place fish on the opposite side of the top grill grate. Cover and cook for 1 hour. Turn fish to other side. If coals have gone out, add a few more pieces of charcoal. For additional smoke flavor, place wet maple, hickory, or apple wood chips, a few at a time, on top of the coals. Fish is done when it flakes easily—2 to 3 hours. Baste fish, if desired, inside and out with barbeque sauce during last 20 minutes of cooking. Debone and serve with crackers as an appetizer.

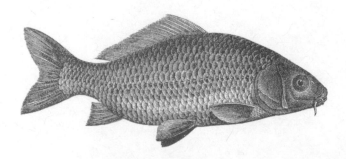

Making a Metal Drum Smoker

One problem with many commercial smokers on the market is that they violate the basic rule of smoke cooking: the heat's too close to what's being smoked. A much better smoker can be made from a 55-gallon drum. These are often used as trash cans at parks, or as containers for oil or other liquids. Ask your city parks department if they have discarded drums, do an online search, or buy one at a farm and home store. Note: Do not use drums or parts made of galvanized steel, as the zinc in it gives off poisonous fumes at high heat. Getting the parts and building this smoker will take you a few hours. But the satisfaction of doing the work yourself—and ending up with a very serviceable product—is well worth the effort. You will need the following:

55-gallon drum, washed and scrubbed clean of any odors
Cold chisel or welder's torch
Drill with 1/4-inch bit
14 1-inch stove bolts with nuts and washer
2 fire grates of slightly smaller diameter than inside of drum;
*   these can be purchased at hardware/farm home stores*
*   or cut from 1/4-inch expanded metal*
Large baking tray or sheet metal, if drum has no cover
4 bricks

If the drum you have comes with a removable cover, set that aside for use later in this project. If the drum has a welded-on cover, remove that by using a welder's torch, cold chisel, or Sawzall. Discard this or keep it for another use (it will likely be too small for a cover). Clean the drum well inside and out with plenty of hot water and soap. There should be no odor remaining in it. Working with whichever tool suits you best (chisel, torch, Sawzall), cut 4 to 6 evenly spaced holes in the bottom of the drum; these should be about 1 inch in diameter and will be used to create draft. Next, cut a rectangular fire door on the outside of the drum a few inches from the bottom. This is where you'll be adding wood, so make the opening big enough—at least 7 by 10 inches. Use two stove bolts (and accompanying nuts and washers) to hinge the cut-away rectangle onto the outside of the drum. Sheet metal can also be used for the door. Next, going around the perimeter of the drum, drill 6 holes 8 inches from the top and 6 holes 8 inches from the bottom of the barrel; install bolts and secure with nuts and washers. Set one fire grate on the bottom bolts; set the other fire grate on the top bolts. If a lid came with the drum, use this as a cover. If the drum came without a cover, use sheet metal, the lid from an old grill, or a baking sheet. Set the smoker so it's resting evenly on bricks. It is now ready for use.

Use natural hardwood charcoal or fragrant wood such as apple, cherry, maple, white oak, or hickory. Allow whatever fuel you are using to burn down to embers before beginning to smoke meat or fish. Adding wood chips helps create extra smoke and flavor. It will take some experimenting to get the feel of cooking with your smoker. More draft occurs when the fire door is left ajar, less when it's shut tight. A piece of green wood set beneath the lid creates draft on top. A good-sized fish, like a salmon or carp, will be smoked in about 2 hours. A grill full of sausages, such as Venison Kielbasa described in the Big Game section of this cookbook, will take about the same amount time. Gamebirds, which should always be cooked skin on, can be larded with bacon or salt pork. Watch these carefully as they are prone to drying out.

PICKLED FISH

Pickling is an effective way to prepare boney fish—like suckers and northern pike—because salt and vinegar break down bones. This recipe works well with any firm-fleshed fish, including bluegills, perch, and bass. Soft-fleshed fish like crappie, catfish, or carp will not hold their texture and should not be used.

> 2 pounds northern pike or sucker fillets cut into chunks
> Brine made from 6 ounces salt and ½ gallon water
> 2 large onions, sliced
> 16 black peppercorns
> 2 cups white vinegar
> 1 cup water
> 1 bunch fresh dill

Prepare brine in large food-grade plastic, metal, or stoneware container; place fish in brine and refrigerate overnight. The next day, drain the fish but do not rinse. Put the fish in a saucepan along with the onion, peppercorns, vinegar, and water. Bring to a boil and turn off immediately. Allow to cool and pack sterilized jars ¾ full, topping with fresh dill. Refrigerate for three days. Fish will keep this way for several weeks. Serve with crackers or rye bread.

Panfried Sheepshead

Sheepshead, or freshwater drum, caught in cool, flowing rivers make for good eating. Avoid those from lakes as their taste is not as good. When filleting sheepshead, remove the skin and the dark stripe of fat found running lengthwise on the fillet. If you like breaded fish, go ahead and use your favorite crumbs or commercial breading. Serve hot, right from the pan.

    1 pound sheepshead fillets
    1 teaspoon seasoning of choice (Old Bay, Cajun, Creole, etc.),
       or more to taste
    Canola oil

Soak fillets in cold salted water for 1 hour prior to cooking. Drain well and blot off all moisture with paper towels. Coat fish liberally, on both sides, with seasoning. In a frying pan, heat oil until just smoking; oil should be about ¼ inch deep. Cook fish 2 minutes per side. Serve with lemon wedges and coleslaw.

Grilled Sturgeon

While sturgeon were once overharvested, their numbers in the Upper Midwest have recovered somewhat thanks to careful management by federal, state, and private conservation efforts. The February spearing season on Wisconsin's Lake Winnebago is the best-known sturgeon fishery in these parts. There are also limited hook-and-line opportunities that vary by state. Sturgeon is a fine-eating fish with firm flesh, like that of swordfish. The flavor, mild and buttery, is enhanced by fresh or dried herbs like parsley, thyme, or tarragon.

1 pound sturgeon steaks
3 tablespoons melted butter
Salt and pepper to taste
1 teaspoon green herb of choice, such as parsley, thyme, tarragon

Preheat grill or broiler. Brush steaks with melted butter, then season with salt, pepper, and herbs. Cook 5 minutes to the side, or until nicely browned outside and flaky inside. Serve hot with lemon wedges and boiled baby red potatoes.

Turtle Soup

The rich and flavorful meat of snapping turtle is great cooked in a soup. The longer it simmers, the more tender it gets. If you harvest the turtle yourself, the meat will still be on the bone. Many commercial fishermen along the Upper Mississippi River sell snapping turtle, both on the bone and boneless. Boneless is easier to deal with. Turtle meat cooked on the bone makes a great broth that adds deep flavor. Take your choice.

1 pound boneless turtle meat, chopped fine,
   or 2 pounds turtle on the bone
2 tablespoons butter
1 bunch of green onions, diced
1 celery stalk, chopped
2 garlic cloves, chopped
¼ cup Italian parsley, chopped
¼ teaspoon thyme
2 tablespoons flour
1 quart chicken broth or turtle broth, hot
Salt and pepper to taste
Dash of hot sauce, or more to taste
½ cup red, white, or sherry wine

If turtle meat is on the bone, cook in 1 quart salted water until meat is tender. Remove meat and strain broth. When meat is cool, strip from bone and cut into small pieces. Keep turtle broth warm on stovetop in a saucepan. If turtle meat is boneless, begin by heating chicken broth in a saucepan. Now, melt butter in the bottom of a large, heavy kettle. Add green onions, celery, garlic, and parsley; cook until vegetables are soft. Dust with flour; add hot broth. Stir well and make sure all flour is absorbed. Add turtle meat and cook until flavors are blended—1 or 2 hours. Add thyme, salt and pepper, hot sauce, and wine. Serve in bowls with crusty French bread on the side. This makes a hearty soup course or a light meal.

Iowa Baked Turtle

Many people don't know that Iowa is full of rivers. In fact, some 20,000 miles of warmwater rivers course through the Hawkeye state. Some are large and well-known—like the Mississippi and Missouri—while others like the Maquoketa, Wapsipinicon, Upper Iowa, Raccoon, Skunk, and Shell are smaller and off the radar. These moist green ribbons provide habitat for migratory birds, fish, and amphibians such as snapping turtles. This recipe for snapping turtle comes to me courtesy of Denny Weiss, who works for the Iowa DNR out of Bellevue, near Dubuque. He uses this two-step process (frying and then moist baking) to get the meat tender. For the record, Denny calls the old saw about seven kinds of turtle meat a myth. In fact, he says, there are only two kinds—dark for the legs and white for the neck and tail.

> 1 cleaned snapping turtle, cut into pieces and trimmed of fat
> Salt and pepper to taste
> Flour for dredging
> Cooking oil
> 1 10-ounce can cream of chicken soup
> 1 10-ounce can cream of mushroom soup

Preheat oven to 350 degrees. Season turtle with salt and pepper and dredge in flour; lightly brown in hot oil. Remove turtle pieces and place in a glass casserole; add soups. Bake, covered, until tender—about 1 hour. Serve over white rice.

CRAWFISH BOIL

Many Upper Midwest lakes and streams have healthy crawfish populations. These little crustaceans taste like lobster, but there's a lot less meat on crawfish than on lobster, so you'll have to catch a bunch for a meal. Check your state's regulations for legal harvest methods and go ahead and trap some. Look for crawfish in cool, rocky-bottomed water. Always keep crawfish alive, in cool water, until you cook them.

1 "catch" of crawfish (1 pound uncooked crawfish
**   per person makes a generous appetizer)**
4 tablespoons Old Bay or fish seasoning of choice
Melted butter or cocktail sauce for dipping

Bring a large kettle of water to a boil; add seasoning. Cook crawfish until they turn bright red, like lobster. Remove from water and drain. Snap tails from bodies; discard bodies. Crack tails and remove meat. Serve crawfish tails with hot drawn butter or cocktail sauce.

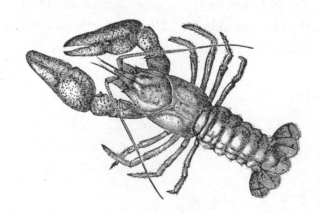

Freshwater Fish Chowder

Folks living in the Midwest need not limit themselves to frozen cod or canned clams for chowder. We have local options that make fine chowder. Firm-fleshed fish, such as pike, walleye, or bass from cold water, work best. Avoid panfish or catfish as their texture doesn't hold up in a soup. If you can track down crawfish tails or turtle meat from a commercial fisherman, add that to the pot.

1 pound fillets from firm, white-fleshed freshwater fish
¼ to ½ pound crawfish tails or turtle meat (optional)
2 cups fish stock
2 tablespoons butter
2 tablespoons flour
1 bunch green onions, chopped
2 celery stalks
¼ teaspoon thyme
1 cup of potatoes, peeled and cubed
¼ cup sherry
2 cups milk, heated

Begin by having 2 cups fish stock hot and ready on the stovetop. You can make stock with the head and filleted carcass of fresh fish, a quart of water, and a chopped onion; cook this until it reduces to half its original volume—about 1 hour. If you're short on time, make stock by dissolving a fish bouillon cube in 2 cups boiling water. In a saucepan that holds at least 2 quarts, melt butter and cook the green onions and celery until soft. Add thyme; sprinkle all with flour. Add stock and blend. Add potatoes and simmer until they are done—about 15 minutes; add sherry, stir. Add milk and mix well. Add fish fillets and cook until they begin to flake apart—about 10 minutes—then add the crawfish or turtle; cook another 5 minutes, or until done. Serve with crusty bread and green salad.

CLEAR RUSSIAN FISH SOUP

Another fish soup recipe? Yes! Soups are a great way to squeeze all the flavor there is from fish. Here we use both the fillets and the carcass that would otherwise be tossed away. This clear soup, called *ukha* in Russian, is a nice change from thick chowders. Making *ukha* is a two-step process—creating the stock and then poaching the fillets and vegetables in that stock—but well worth the effort.

> 2 pounds fish trimmings (what's left, minus entrails,
>   after filleting) of white-fleshed fish such as bass, crappie,
>   perch, walleye, or northern pike
> 1 onion, sliced
> ½ cup chopped parsley, including stems
> 1 teaspoon salt
> 6 whole black peppercorns
> 2 quarts water
> 1 pound salmon fillets, cut into serving-size pieces
> 2 potatoes, peeled and cubed
> 2 carrots, peeled and chopped
> Fresh dill to taste
> Salt and pepper to taste

Add fish trimmings and next five ingredients to a deep kettle; cook for ½ hour, then strain stock through a sieve. Return the stock to the pan in which it was cooked or another large, deep pan. Add potato and carrot; cook until soft. Add fish fillets and cook until they begin to break apart. Correct seasoning, if necessary, with salt and pepper. Serve sprinkled with fresh cut dill in bowls. Rye or black bread with plenty of butter— and, of course, chilled vodka—is all you need to make this a meal.

WHITEFISH CAVIAR WITH BLINI

Whitefish caviar is a very affordable delicacy made from the eggs of whitefish living in the cold waters of Lakes Superior and Michigan. You can buy it for $10 or $15 a pound, which wouldn't even get you a half-ounce of traditional Russian caviar. To make whitefish caviar, commercial fishermen harvest eggs from female whitefish in fall and then cure them in salt brine. If you're close to Lake Michigan or Superior, chances are you can find a commercial fisherman who sells it. Those living farther inland can order from fishmarkets such as Peterson's in Hancock, Michigan, or Bodin's in Bayfield, Wisconsin. There are a number of ways to eat caviar, but my favorite is with Russian pancakes known as *blini*. Top blini with sour cream and a spoonful of whitefish caviar, chase them down with a shot of chilled vodka, and you'll be enjoying some of the finest eating possible. Blini are traditionally eaten at celebratory events, such as the week prior to Lent, known as Maslenitsa, or Butter Festival. Buckwheat flour can be purchased at food co-ops or in the natural foods section of larger grocery stores.

1½ cups lukewarm milk
½ package (½ tablespoon) active dry yeast
3 eggs, beaten, at room temperature
½ teaspoon salt
1 tablespoon sugar
4 tablespoons melted butter
1 cup white flour
½ cup buckwheat flour

In a large mixing bowl, dissolve yeast in milk and let stand until foamy; add beaten eggs. Add remaining ingredients and mix until blended. Allow to sit in a warm, draft-free place, such as an unlit oven, for at least 2 hours. Drop 1 tablespoon of batter at a time on a hot skillet or griddle. Fry on both sides, as you would a regular pancake. Keep in a warm oven until ready to serve. Serve with sour cream, whitefish caviar, and melted butter.

Caviar in a Half-Pound Tub? You Betcha!

As I was tracking down foods for a special meatless Christmas Eve dinner, I found myself on the phone with Bodin Fisheries of Washburn, Wisconsin, way up on Lake Superior. I didn't think there was any way I could afford the local whitefish caviar advertised on their website. But why not ask how much if only, as they say, for giggles? I held the line as the clerk checked. There was a long pause and the noises you might imagine from a fish market—clangs, shouts, shuffling around. Then came the answer.

"Five dollars for a half-pound tub."

Now, I couldn't figure out what to say, exactly, but a number of things came to mind. First, I thought they were joking. But when I considered I was talking to fishermen who go out on Lake Superior in the middle of winter, I figured this was no joke. My next thought was to buy everything they had in stock, work on my Russian accent, and sell the stuff from the back of a van in Chicago or Milwaukee. This seemed like an option, but I realized I hadn't tried the caviar yet. And so, coming to my senses, I ordered five tubs. It arrived the next day, packed on dry ice.

Now, I'm a writer and supposed to be good with words. I've had some pretty good meals over the years—paella in the south of Spain, fresh salmon in Scotland, briny lobster in Maine, venison cooked juicy-rare over wood coals, even a dollop of good caviar now and then at fancy weddings. How else can I say it? I was blown away by whitefish caviar! There was the novelty of eating caviar at cod fillet prices. But it was more than that. Here was a perfect balance of taste, texture, and color. Salty and sweet, crisp and juicy with a nutty aftertaste, and a rich yellow-gold hue. All this *and* it comes from our own clear, cold Great Lakes—with no fussy tins, Romanoff logo, or European pretense.

We ate a lot of caviar that Christmas—on black bread, in omelets with cream cheese, with blini, chased with vodka, and straight up. The good news is that whitefish populations in Lake Superior remain fairly stable—and whitefish caviar prices have only increased modestly. You can buy whitefish caviar or herring caviar from a number of fish markets along Lake Superior and Lake Michigan; it's available fresh in fall and sometimes frozen in winter. Among these fish markets are Peterson's in Michigan's Upper Peninsula; Great Lakes Gold in Sturgeon Bay and Bodin's Fisheries on Lake Superior in Wisconsin; and Dockside or Russ Kendall's on Minnesota's Lake Superior coast. If you're too far to make the drive, check them out online. Many shops will ship to you on dry ice. Next time someone tells you that you have to travel to the coasts or Europe to get gourmet food, tell them you'll pass. You've got your own caviar—and it comes in a half-pound tub.

Other Ways to Serve Whitefish Caviar

With sour cream or butter on top of blini is one way to present whitefish caviar. Following are a few other suggestions.

As a filling for a fluffy cream-cheese omelet
On black bread topped with sour cream, dill, and red onion
Mix caviar into cooked egg yolks and mayonnaise, 2 tablespoons for every
   dozen hardboiled eggs
With chilled vodka shots

BAKED NORTHERN PIKE

One reason to appreciate northern pike is that they're common in the Upper Midwest. You'll find them in weedy bays of northern lakes or in backwaters of large river systems. Size and bag limits are usually liberal, so no worries about keeping a few pike. Smaller pike can be pickled or used in soup. Don't worry about the bones. Below is a way to deal with them.

> 1 northern pike (4 pounds or larger)
> Salt and pepper to taste
> 2 tablespoons melted butter
> Fresh lemon juice to taste
> Dill to taste (optional)

Fillet the pike as follows to produce five boneless fillets. Scale the fish, but leave the head on. (If you prefer fillets with the skin off, then skip scaling and remove skin after fillets have been cut from fish.) The first fillet is located between the back of the head and the dorsal fin, parallel to the belly. For this fillet, make a cut behind the head up to, but not through, the backbone. If you hear blade on bone, bring the knife up a bit. Now turn the knife 90 degrees and run it along—again, not through or into—the backbone until you reach the dorsal fin. Fillet out the Y bones running through the center of this piece. The next two fillets run between the gills and dorsal fin, on either side of the fish. On one side of the fish, run the knife along the rib bones from gills to dorsal; repeat on other side. You should now have three fillets. The remaining two fillets are located between the dorsal fin and tail, again on either side of the fish. Cut these off the fish and you will now have five fillets.

Preheat grill or oven to medium-hot, around 350 degrees. Season fillets with salt, pepper, melted butter, lemon juice, and optional dill. Cook on a clean oiled grill or broiler pan until fish just begins to flake—about 15 minutes. You can also pan-fry pike fillets in oil in a hot skillet. Serve with boiled potatoes and asparagus or green beans.

WILD EDIBLES

Except in the dead of winter, there's always something to forage in the Upper Midwest. As the angler in these parts needs to decide whether to chase Great Lakes salmon, Northwoods walleye, or spring creek trout—and the hunter must zero in on grouse, deer, or waterfowl—so the forager has a veritable treasure trove to comb through. Watercress, asparagus, morel mushrooms? Strawberries, raspberries, blackberries? Hickory nuts, hazelnuts, oyster mushrooms? Just remembering what is coming up when can be a challenge. Traditional societies the world over have come up with a solution for this—a calendar stick. If you happen to be bumming around northeast Iowa some time, stop in at the Vesterheim Norwegian-American Museum in Decorah. The calendar stick they have on display is two-sided, about three feet long, and dates back to the late eighteenth century. What really stands out are the carvings—religious and agricultural symbols for each day of the year. There's something direct and larger-than-life about these forms. And it makes you think someone needs to create a calendar stick for today's Upper Midwest forager, to help keep track of what wildfoods are coming into season.

At any rate, I'll do my best to create a calendar stick in print. Just as the forms on the stick at Vesterheim are approximations, bear in mind that emergence dates given here are also ballpark. In recent years, there's been a trend toward earlier springs and later, warmer falls. And of course emergence varies by location. Morel mushrooms in the southern part of the region may begin popping up in April; in far northern reaches, they may be a month behind this. Even if it's approximate, I hope this helps readers get at the embarrassment of our natural riches.

Spring

About the first wild harvest in these parts is watercress. A close relation to the nasturtium flower—whose Latin name translates to "nose turner"—pungent watercress is an import from Europe that's become naturalized in North America's cold waters. There's a great deal of it growing in Driftless-area Wisconsin, Iowa, and Minnesota. It seems to love the limestone-rich waters here. While this may be a hotspot for watercress, you can find it in nearly any farm country spring or trout stream. As with many plants, the earliest growth of watercress is the most tender. Harvest young plants in March and April. Rinse them well of any sand or snails. Collect it from clean waters. Watercress goes well in salads, sautéed as a green, or even in place of Chinese cabbage in eggrolls or stir-fries. I enjoy it, raw or quickly cooked, as a side for fresh trout.

Everyone is waiting for the magic word—*morel mushrooms*, or just *mushrooms* as they're known in Wisconsin—so let's get to it. When do they emerge? Like many phenological events, there's been a trend in recent years toward earlier rather than later. Talking about morels in April may seem hasty. But, with recent mild winters and early springs, I've heard of finds as early as mid-April in southern Wisconsin and Iowa. Now, that was the spring of 2012, which was the warmest on record. But still, depending on the spring and your location, it's good to start picturing the first tiny grays in your mind when the first warm days of April roll around. Look for them in mid-May in Michigan's UP, far-northern Wisconsin, and Minnesota. What triggers morels to pop up is ground temperature—and moisture. Begin to look on south-facing slopes after a warm rain. Poke around newly dead elm trees and live or dead apple trees. If you have access to an abandoned apple orchard, even better. Streambeds and old railroad grades as well as clearings in the woods are also productive. As the season gets on, morels begin to emerge on north-facing slopes as well. When the mushrooms get big—6 inches or more—and light in color, the season's winding up.

Cut morels at ground level with pocketknife or snap them with your fingers. Leave the root of the mushroom in the ground as it may continue to produce. I carry a small burlap bag to carry mushrooms; any breathable fabric with small holes will do. Plastic bags are fine if your mushrooms are going right in the refrigerator or fry pan; storage in plastic in warm or wet weather, though, can cause your mushrooms to get mushy. To make sure it's a morel and not a false morel, cut the mushroom in half lengthwise. It should be hollow; if there is any solid or cottony material inside, discard the mushroom immediately because you've likely found a false morel. You can soak morels in cold salt water—make sure to drain them well before cooking or wipe them with a paper towel. They go well with scrambled eggs, chicken, game, and asparagus. Nothing beats fresh morels, salted and peppered, sautéed in butter. Lots of butter.

In my mind, you can't mention morels without mentioning asparagus. They both pop up around the same time. If you can harvest fresh trout and a wild turkey along with your morels and asparagus, then you're really in business. I've heard this called the King's Quartet by a local farmer and I'd have to agree—it's springtime's best. Wild asparagus has many of the same preferences as morel mushrooms. They both like partial sun and well-drained soil. If you know of an old asparagus farm or patch—Michigan is a big asparagus producer—where you have permission to go, have at it. Asparagus seeds often get trapped in fencerows, so these are another good spot, as are roadside ditches. Other times, I've found isolated stands of asparagus growing in woodlots and along streambanks for no apparent reason. The seeds must have traveled there and taken root. Finding these tiny spears in thick cover is tough work. Keep a look out for ferny stalks as you're driving by. These stalks are too tough to eat, but they're a sign of a healthy asparagus patch. In summer and fall, look for the yellowed stalks of asparagus gone to seed and return for good picking the following spring. Always get permission before you enter private land.

Harvest only the tender part of the asparagus plant. These should snap off easily. If it's hard to break, the plant's too old—don't bother with it. Rinse the spears well, and use them within a few days. Gently steamed asparagus is the best way to go for the year's first find. Douse it with salt, pepper, and butter. Asparagus can also be grilled, sautéed, cooked in a risotto or paella, or browned and added to a scramble.

SUMMER

There's no question about it: summer's about berries for the Upper Midwest forager. Strawberries, raspberries, blackcaps, blackberries, and blueberries. There's a bear in each of us that comes out during berry season. If winter's about hunkering down and spring about the earth's first new shoots, then summer's about bright and sweet things hanging from bushes. There's something in the mammal brain that sees the berries and wants to gorge. And for good reason. They taste great and are full of vitamins.

Wild strawberries are the first berries to emerge in these parts. They don't keep well, but they are uncommonly sweet. Eat them on the spot or bring a handful back to the cabin to top pancakes or yogurt. Look for them on forest paths, along roadsides, and in sandy-soil clearings. Their short season is around Memorial Day in the southern part of the region and into June further north. Like the Ingmar Bergman film of the same title, wild strawberries are about fleeting pleasures. In a way, they are more a harbinger—a sign—than a thing in themselves. They hint at what's to come. Don't worry about canning or pies. Don't hoard them. Gorge on them. Inhale them. They won't last.

Following strawberries are red and black raspberries, from late June to mid-July. Red raspberries are domestic strains that have established themselves in the wild—likely around an abandoned orchard or farm. These are great eating but don't frequent a specific habitat, other than being strongly associated with human settlement. If you find them, use them for pie, in jam, or over ice cream. Black raspberries—or blackcaps—emerge around the Fourth of July. Blackcaps are widespread throughout the woodlands of the Upper Midwest. Of all bramblefruits, I believe black raspberries have the most intense flavor. It's at once intensely sweet and quite tart. You bite into one and your eyes almost water. Look for blackcap patches that are in partial shade, or growing near water, as they produce the juiciest berries. Check along the sides of roads, especially logging roads. If an area has been newly burned, as happens at public hunting grounds undergoing habitat work, this is a good place to look. Unlike red raspberries, the core of black raspberries remains on the fruit. Black raspberries make first-rate jam. They're great over vanilla ice cream, too. Black raspberry cobbler is the perfect dessert to accompany a summer fish fry. On the downside, they can be seedy and dry out easily. Pick only big, moist berries.

Blackberries emerge in early August and can grow well into September. There's an abandoned railroad grade where I pass-shoot doves in early September. I've often come back with a sack full of blackberries and brace of doves. I like this because I'm doing double-duty, and also because I'm straddling two seasons—the end of summer berries and the beginning of fall gamebirds. In addition to their timing, blackberries differ from raspberries in their size—the former being about the size of a quarter while the latter are usually the size of a dime or smaller. Also blackberry canes are just plain huge, sometimes ten feet tall or more, and really thorny. Picking them can require a cost-benefit analysis. How much blood am I willing to lose for a cache of blackberries? While not as piquant as black raspberries, blackberries have their own wine-like sweetness and can be really plentiful. Find the right spot and gallons can be yours. A popular Northwoods berry picking rig is a gallon milk jug—cut off at the top—worn on a string around the neck. The hands are free to work. And swat mosquitoes. And pull thorns from your flesh. Wear long pants and long sleeves, but you'll still get scratched up.

Blueberries are not a bramblefruit, but they are, sure enough, a berry. They grow in great quantities in the sandy soils of Michigan as well those of northern Wisconsin and Minnesota. As with many berries, blueberries are fond of water, making lakeshores, bogs, and riverbottoms prime habitat for them. Minnesota's North Shore—specifically, the Boundary Waters and Gunflint Trail—are fine blueberry country, as are the many public forests of Upper Michigan and northern Wisconsin. The fruit is purple-blue and grows on low, thornless bushes, ripening in July and August. I must confess that I've never developed the mania for blueberries that I have for bramblefruits. This is probably more a statement about the author—who lives outside of prime blueberry range—than the fruit itself. Blueberries are good in pancakes (especially buttermilk pancakes), over ice cream, and in syrups and jams.

A few other summer wild fruits bear mentioning—wild grapes, gooseberries, various shrubs, and mulberries. These don't rate on the same level as the berries discussed earlier, but they do have specialized uses and are worth harvesting if you have a plan in mind. Wild grape, sometimes called river grapes, grows on thick vines in shaded, moist places. You'll find them growing along fencerows, streambanks, and riverbottoms. I've often found islands on the Wisconsin and Mississippi Rivers where the dominant plant was wild grape. They ripen in late August and September and make fine jam and jelly. My attempts at winemaking using them have been nothing short of disaster—with one bottle exploding above the Easter ham and painting the white ceiling purple—so you'll have to look elsewhere for a wild grape wine recipe. Gooseberries, which also like moist terrain, are used both unripe (green) and ripe (purple-black); pies and jams are their chief destination and they are quite tart, like a black currant. The fruits of elderberry trees, chokecherry trees, and sand cherry bushes ripen in July and August and are used chiefly for jam. Mulberries, which are a European import that's become established in the U.S., ripen in June and July. They're worth mentioning because they are common to the point of being a nuisance. But my friend Cecilia O'Brien—of the ever-resourceful Johnson family of Soldiers Grove, Wisconsin—has shown me how to transform them into a tasty pancake syrup. Send the kids out to fill buckets. Boil the berries. Strain, thicken with sugar, and there's your syrup. No pesky hulling required.

FALL

Fall has its own special wildfoods. There's wild rice; mushrooms such as oyster, puffball, and sulfur shelf; hickory nuts, walnuts, hazelnuts. In addition, there are wild plums and wild apples. There's so much going on, it can be tricky to fit it all in with bow hunting, walleye and steelhead fishing, upland bird hunting, and duck hunting. It's a tough job, as they say, but someone has to do it.

Wild rice, or *Zizania palustris*, is a grass that occurs naturally in slow-moving rivers and shallow lakes of the Upper Midwest. It grows from tall stalks or canes rooted in shallow water; these canes in turn support clusters of seeds, which fall from the plant into the water in autumn and are a favorite food of waterfowl. Wild rice has also been a source of spiritual and physical sustenance for Native people for thousands of years because it is tasty, portable, nutritious, and versatile. When European settlers arrived in the region, they saw how valuable it was and soon incorporated it into their own diet. Wild rice is harvested in the early part of September. In Native—particularly Ojibwe—communities, elders known as rice chiefs determine the start of each rice season. Shallow-draft canoes, skiffs, and jon boats are the typical ricing boats; a team of two ricers in the boat carries out ricing duties. Typically, the person seated in the stern paddles or navigates with a pushpole. The person seated in the bow gently strokes the rice grains from the long stalks of the plant into the hull of the boat. When a sufficient quantity is gathered—when the boat can hold no more or if the team decides to call it quits—the ricers head to shore. There, the rice is stored in baskets, roasted, and then dried. Check your state's regulations governing wild rice before attempting to harvest it. Most wild rice used commercially today comes from cultivated wild rice paddies, where harvesting is mechanized.

For my money, there's no finer nut to be found anywhere than wild hickory nuts. Now, the Upper Midwest sits at the northern edge of hickory range, but there's still a good belt of hickory habitat across the southern half of the region—lower Michigan, southern Wisconsin, Iowa, and southern Minnesota. Hickory trees favor the same kind of sunny, well-drained habitat as burr oaks, and can often be found growing among them. Only the nuts of shagbark hickories are eaten; nuts from the bitternut or yellowbud hickory tree are bitter. The more pronounced bark of the shagbark—and better taste of the nuts!—make it easy to tell them apart. I start to gather hickory nuts at the start of small game season—the second week in September—and that should be pretty constant throughout the region. A green outer shell encases the nutshell, and the nutmeat in turn surrounds the meat. You can gather these anytime until the snow falls. But expect competition from squirrels, which also love hickory nuts.

And for good reason. If you've never had a hickory nut, imagine the flavor of pecan, reduced and intensified by several orders of magnitude, and fortified by a sweet smokiness. By way of analogy, the pecan is to the hickory nut as the button mushroom is to the morel mushroom: a pale comparison. The bad news about hickory nuts is that they're hard to shell. Hard is an understatement. They're awful. A lot of tedious work. Hammer and vice. Special nutcracker. Sitting on the floor over spread-out newspaper. There's no quick way to do it. The only easy way is expensive: buy them at a farmers' market in hickory country. Once you have them shelled, however, the fun begins. Sauté them in butter and spread them over pancakes. Use them as you would almonds in almondine sauces—over fish or vegetables. Tuck them into muffins or cookies. Add them to sweet breads. A true hickory nut aficionado I know makes them into a delicious, rich butter. Once hulled and shelled, hickory nuts will keep for a year or more in an airtight container. Left too long, however, they develop a bitter taste. Since they're expensive (in money or time), it's best to use them fresh.

Hazelnuts run a close second to hickory nuts. The intensity isn't there, but hazelnuts have their own mild, buttery flavor. Once very common throughout the Midwest, hazelnuts are, sadly, less so now. Fencerow-to-fencerow farming has reduced their habitat. Still, you can find them along ditches and hedgerows in the country. As with hickory nuts, you know they are ready to pick when they start falling from the tree. And again, as with hickory nuts, the critters are very fond of them—squirrels, grouse, pheasant, and quail—so it's best to pick them when you see them. Hazelnut trees, or bushes, are 9 to 12 feet in height. The nuts ripen in August and September. Hazelnuts are suited to all the things a pecan or hickory is nut is suited to, including baked goods, sautéed and served over pancakes, in sauces, or put through a food mill and made into butter. Beechnuts are the fruit of beech trees, which grow in the northern part of the region. They're a favorite food of grouse—and often harvested by grouse hunters—and can be used in place of pecans or hazelnuts.

Last, we come to the black walnut. Common in the southern part of our region, walnut trees are nothing if not widespread—from city parks to suburban neighborhoods, from woodlots to shelterbelts. In addition to being widespread, the amount of nutmeats they produce is impressive. Nuts drop from the trees in July and can be harvested any time after that. As with other nuts, there is some work to be done to get at the nutmeat. The outer green hull must first be removed, the nutshell cracked and opened, and the nutmeat coaxed out. Black walnuts are oilier and have a stronger flavor than their domestic counterparts grown commercially in California and England. If the somewhat sharp taste of domestic walnuts appeals to you, you'll probably like black walnuts. If, like me, you don't care for the domestic variety, don't bother with the wild ones. Walnuts are a favorite add-in to chocolate products, brownies among them. They also find their place in cookies, breads, and sprinkled over oatmeal.

The mere mention of wild mushrooms will send some fleeing. Rest assured, however, that we include here only safe, easy-to-identify mushroom varieties. In addition, all would-be mushroomers are advised to purchase a quality field guide to mushrooms before going out picking—and to discard any mushroom they cannot positively identify. The easiest of the fall mushrooms is the giant puffball. Technically an earthball and not a mushroom, these big, white specimens are commonly seen growing on lawns or in the woods in late summer and early fall. At a distance they may look like a white kickball or soccer ball. Look for specimens that are firm and white, inside and out, and larger than your fist. Avoid puffballs that have begun to yellow; these are no longer fresh. Cut into all puffballs perpendicular to the mushroom—there should be no outline of developing mushroom inside. If you find this, discard the mushroom because it's not a puffball. Puffballs are good cooked with scrambled eggs, added to spaghetti sauce, or made into fritters. Refrigerate and use puffballs within a few days of finding.

Another common fall and early winter mushroom is the oyster mushroom. You may or may not have noticed these while walking through the woods, but you've almost certainly seen them in grocery stores and farmers' market over the last few years, as their cultivation has become more widespread. There are three distinguishing characteristics of an oyster mushroom in the wild: it has gills, it grows from a stump or log, and is found in summer, fall, or early winter. All mushrooms with these characteristics are in the pleuroryte family and are edible. Oyster mushrooms grow in moist woodlands. They can be grayish, buff or yellow, or white in color. They pair beautifully with fowl and take to white wine nicely. They're also tasty simply sautéed in butter with salt and pepper and a squeeze of lemon. I've supplemented many a waterfowl and small game hunt coming out of the woods with oyster mushrooms—sometimes even several pounds of them, as they tend to grow in clusters. Oyster mushrooms can be dried in a dehydrator, in the oven on a low temperature, or threaded through with a string and allowed to dry that way. Use fresh oyster mushrooms within a few days; store dried oyster mushrooms in sealed glass jars.

Sulfur shelf mushrooms, sometimes called chicken of the woods, are another fall mushroom that grows in Upper Midwest woodlands. Like the oyster mushroom, the sulfur shelf attaches itself to a host tree and grows out in bracket fashion. The good news about a find of sulfur shelf is it's a prolific mushroom. "Shelves" may be as large as 16 inches in diameter; many such shelves tend to grow from one or several host logs. The sulfur shelf's texture is like chamois or smooth leather and color can range from a pale yellow to a dull orange. The taste of the sulfur shelf is similar to chicken. It pairs well with pheasant, grouse, or turkey; some cooks even use it as a chicken substitute. As with many other mushrooms, sulfur shelf is equally delicious sautéed in butter or olive oil with a bit or parsley, salt, and pepper. Use sulfur shelf mushrooms within a few days of harvesting. Young specimens are best for eating; wipe them clean with a damp paper towel. Sulfur shelf mushrooms are not typically dried.

Rounding out the list of fall wild edibles are wild plums. Perhaps the best way to find wild plums in fall is to look for the white or pink blossoms in spring. Then, make a note and come back around Labor Day. You can make a good jelly or jam from wild plums; just follow your favorite jam recipe, using about ¾ cup sugar for every cup of clean, washed, seeded fruit. Cook until the fruit sticks to the back of spoon and store the jam in clean, sterilized jars. A few wild plums added to the bottom of the roaster, alongside waterfowl or upland gamebirds, adds a special piquancy.

Blintzes with Fresh Berries

Blintzes, like pierogi, are a mainstay of Eastern European cooking that have found a permanent seat at the American table. My Ukrainian grandmother called these thin, unraised pancakes *blinchiki*, but I use the term *blintz* here because it will be familiar to most readers. Blintzes keep well for a few days in the refrigerator. To freeze, separate individual pancakes with sheets of wax paper, and enclose stacks in freezer paper or ziplock bags.

Pancakes
3 tablespoons clarified butter
1 ⅓ cups white flour
1 tablespoon sugar
¼ teaspoon salt
1 cup milk at room temperature
3 eggs, beaten
½ cup plain seltzer water

Fillings
2 cups fresh-picked berries, washed and sprinkled with sugar
2 cups soft farmers cheese (called *tvrog* in Slavic markets) or ricotta cheese, seasoned with 1 tablespoon sugar, 1 teaspoon lemon juice, and ½ cup yellow raisins
1 cup whipped cream or whole-milk yogurt
1 cup jam

Preheat oven to warm. Clarify butter by pouring melted butter through a sieve and into a bowl. In a separate large bowl, mix together dry ingredients; add milk and eggs. Mix until very smooth—no lumps remaining. Let batter stand 10 minutes. Mix in seltzer water. Heat 7- or 8-inch skillet (nonstick or well-seasoned cast iron) on stovetop; brush with clarified butter. A drop of water should now "dance" in the skillet. Add 2 tablespoons of batter to the skillet and tilt so it covers the entire bottom of pan. When edges curl, flip blintz and cook briefly on second side—perhaps 10 seconds. Repeat until batter is used up. Keep cooked blintzes on a plate in warm oven. Serve with fillings.

Buttermilk Pancakes with Berries

While some people prefer thin, unraised crepes, others favor fluffy old-fashioned pancakes. And if you're making homemade pancakes, why not go that extra step and make them with buttermilk? Tangy buttermilk and sweet berries make for a perfect marriage. Remember not to over-beat the batter—a few lumps will do no harm. Also, this recipe calls for placing berries *onto* the pancakes while cooking, not stirring them into the batter. This keeps the berries from gushing all over the skillet and making a mess.

1 cup flour
Oil or butter for greasing skillet
1 teaspoon salt
1 teaspoon baking powder
1 tablespoon sugar
1 egg, beaten
1¼ cups buttermilk
3 tablespoons butter, melted and cooled
1 cup fresh berries (blueberries, blackberries, black raspberries)

Preheat skillet or griddle on stovetop on medium-high heat; grease with oil or butter. In a large bowl, mix together flour, salt, sugar, and baking powder. Add the egg, buttermilk, and butter. Mix together just until all the dry ingredients are moistened. Do not overmix or pancakes will be tough. Add ¼ cup of batter to skillet. When bottom is golden-brown and top begins to bubble, gently place a few berries into the top side of the pancake. Flip and cook on the other side until done. Repeat until all batter is used. Serve with maple syrup, butter, and additional fresh berries on the side.

Berry Jam

Berries are one of those feast-or-famine foods. In summer, they're so abundant you pick them by the pail or flat. Scatter them over cereal, sprinkle them on ice cream, or just eat them by the handful—you just can't use them up. But in winter, when there's only pale fruit from the southern hemisphere available, you'd give your eye teeth for just a few. So make some jam. You'll be glad you did when you reach in the back of the cupboard on one of those minus-10 degree nights and find a bit of summer preserved.

4 cups berries (hulled and washed)
3 cups sugar
4 hot, sterilized Mason jars plus bands and lids, or more as needed

Place berries in the bottom of a heavy saucepan; smash them down a bit so they release their juices. Add sugar and cook on low flame until jam sticks to the back of a spoon. This will take between 15 and 30 minutes. Pour into sterilized jars, put on bands and lids, and hot jam will cause jars to seal.

Cecilia O'Brien's Mulberry Syrup

Mulberries are super-abundant in June and July, and not bad to eat. But that's just it—they're *not bad*. I'd always felt there was a way to get more flavor out of them, but got bogged down with the idea of dealing with those pesky stems. The answer to my mulberry question came one June evening as my wife and I were sitting on the back porch at the home of our friends, Joe and Cecilia O'Brien, in southwest Wisconsin. The trees on the bluffs behind them swayed, and the light of evening was just coming on. It was also the height of mulberry season and one of their lovely children had just picked a bucketful. When Cecilia explained these were destined for syrup, my ears perked up. And when I heard there was no stem-pulling or pectin involved, I got out my notebook double-time. Here was the perfect way to deal with mulberries: amping up their flavor with minimal work. Mulberry syrup is great, served warmed, over French toast or pancakes with some crisp sausage or bacon on the side.

    1 quart fresh-picked mulberries, rinsed
    1 cup of sugar, or more as needed

Put mulberries and sugar and in a heavy saucepan. Cook down until berries are reduced to a loose syrup. Put through a strainer; discard solids and return strained syrup to pan. Cook, stirring occasionally, until syrup reaches desired consistency. Test and add more sugar if you like it sweeter. Store in sterilized jars and refrigerate. You can also freeze mulberry syrup as you would containers of freezer jam.

BLACK CURRANT VODKA

The currant patch in our front yard is one of our prized possessions. We use the red ones for jam and game sauces and the black ones for flavoring baked goods and liquors. For a refreshing summertime drink, mix black currant vodka—one part to five—with pink lemonade, squeeze in a lime wedge, and serve over ice. Currants are ripe in late June or early July. Look for them at farmers' markets or specialty stores. Blackberries or black raspberries will also work in this recipe.

1 liter good-quality vodka
2 cups black currants
1 cup sugar or ¾ cup honey
1-quart Mason jar with lid

Wash currants well and remove any pieces of vine. Place them in the Mason jar with sugar or honey and shake or stir until well mixed. Add vodka to level full. Allow to sit for several months. Serve as an after-dinner drink or with your favorite mixer.

Classic Cobbler

Cobblers are great way to use seasonal fruit, whether berries, apples, rhubarb, peaches, cherries, or a combination of these goodies. Apples and peaches can be cooked skin-on or skin-off, according to your taste.

> 5 cups washed fruit (berries should be hulled, cherries pitted,
>   and apples and peaches sliced)
> 1 cup brown or white sugar
> 1 stick of butter at room temperature, cut into pieces;
>   reserve the wrapper
> ¾ cup flour
> ¼ teaspoon salt

Preheat oven to 350 degrees. With wrapper from butter stick, grease the bottom of a 9-inch pie pan. Add fruit; sprinkle with water. Cream together the sugar, butter, flour, and salt. Spread on top of fruit. Bake until topping is golden brown and fruit is bubbling—30 to 45 minutes. Serve topped with ice cream or whipped cream. For a big crowd, double the recipe and serve in a shallow baking dish about 16 by 9 inches.

Johnsons' Hickory Nut Pie

This recipe comes from my friends the Johnsons, who live on a small farm in Crawford County, Wisconsin, near my cabin. Their woods, like many in the southern tier of the Upper Midwest, has a good population of hickory trees. Being resourceful farmers (kind of redundant, isn't it?), the Johnsons adapted a pecan pie recipe from *Bon Appétit* to these delicious nuts. Now, shelling and hulling takes some work—or money if you can find shelled hickory nuts at a farmers' market—and the recipe is a bit involved. But the results are well, well worth it. Earthy hickory nuts and pungent bourbon work magic on the taste buds.

To toast hickory nuts, bake them on a tray in a 350-degree oven for 10 minutes, or cook them in a large skillet, with just enough butter to moisten, for 5 minutes.

> 1 9-inch pie crust (store-bought or home-made)
> 1 cup brown sugar
> 1 cup light corn syrup
> ¼ cup unsalted butter, melted
> 3 large eggs
> 4 tablespoons bourbon
> 1 teaspoon vanilla extract
> ¼ teaspoon salt
> 2 cups hickory nuts, toasted
> 1 cup whipping cream, chilled
> 2 tablespoons sugar

Place pie crust in a deep glass pie dish. Refrigerate 1 hour. (If using pre-baked crust, skip to the next paragraph and fill crust as directed.) Preheat oven to 375. Line crust with foil and fill with dried beans or pie weights. Bake until crust edges begin to brown and crust is set, about 17 minutes. Remove foil and weights. Bake until golden brown, pressing with back of fork if crust bubbles, about 5 minutes longer. Transfer pie crust to rack. Maintain oven temperature.

Whisk brown sugar, corn syrup, and melted butter in large bowl to blend. Whisk in eggs one at a time. Stir in 3 tablespoons bourbon, vanilla, salt, and then toasted hickory nuts. Pour filling into prepared crust. Bake pie until edges puff and center is just set, about 50 minutes. Cool pie on rack at least 1 hour. (Can be made 6 hours ahead. Let stand at room temperature.)

Using electric mixer, beat 1 cup chilled whipping cream, 2 tablespoons sugar, and remaining 1 tablespoon bourbon in large bowl until cream holds peaks. Serve pie warm or at room temperature with bourbon cream.

HICKORY NUT BROWNIES

Following a brownie recipe is easy. Shelling hickory nuts is the hard part. A hammer and vice or nutcracker and pick—plus a heaping tablespoon of patience—is what you'll need. Once you taste brownies made with hickory nuts, though, you'll see that your time was well spent. If you have a favorite brownie recipe, feel free to substitute it.

    1 stick of butter, melted
    1 teaspoon vanilla extract
    ½ cup all-purpose flour
    ¼ teaspoon baking powder
    1 cup hickory nuts
    1 cup sugar
    2 eggs, beaten
    ⅓ cup cocoa
    ¼ teaspoon salt

Heat oven to 350 degrees and grease and flour a 9-inch baking pan. In a large bowl, combine butter, sugar, and vanilla; add eggs. Sift together flour, cocoa, baking powder, and salt; add to egg mixture and mix until blended. Stir in nuts. Spread into baking pan. Bake 20 to 25 minutes. These can be frosted, if you like, once cooled.

Basic Wild Rice

If there's one go-to game side dish in the Upper Midwest, it's wild rice. The nutty, rich flavor is the perfect accompaniment to waterfowl, as many ducks and geese passing through the area have been feeding in wild rice beds. As a counterpoint to white-meat gamebirds such as pheasant and grouse, it hits the right note. It's also a complement to big game, such as deer and moose, and small game, such as rabbit and squirrel. But the appeal of wild rice goes beyond the culinary sphere. It's been a staple household and commercial item of the Upper Midwest—where it grows both wild and cultivated in shallow, marshy waters—for centuries. Long before Europeans set foot on the continent, wild rice was a physical and spiritual mainstay of the Native people here—and it continues to be so today.

1 carrot, peeled and chopped
1 celery stalk, chopped
½ bunch green onions, chopped
½ cup mushrooms, chopped, or more to taste
1 garlic clove, chopped
2 tablespoons chicken, turkey, or goose fat (or butter) for sautéing
3 cups chicken or beef stock, hot
¼ teaspoon dried thyme, or more to taste
Salt and pepper to taste
1 cup uncooked wild rice

Melt fat in the bottom of a large saucepan or kettle. In it, cook carrot, celery, green onions, mushrooms, and garlic. Add hot stock and then rice. Turn up heat and bring to a full boil. Add salt and pepper until broth tastes right. Reduce heat, cover, and cook for 45 minutes or until kernels soften. Remove lid, fluff with fork, and serve hot. I use beef stock for richer-flavored meats like waterfowl, venison, and rabbit. Chicken stock works well with the lighter taste of pheasant, grouse, and squirrel. For a richer side dish, cook ½-pound of bulk pork sausage with the vegetables and leave in as the rice cooks.

Wild Rice Quiche

This delicious recipe comes from the Great Lakes Indian Fish and Wildlife Commission, which governs the use of natural resources for Indian tribes living in the western Great Lakes region. This quiche makes a terrific brunch or dinner dish, especially on a cold day.

3 eggs, beaten
1½ cups half-and-half
¾ cup Swiss cheese, grated
¾ cup Monterey Jack cheese, grated
3 green onions, chopped
1 tablespoon flat leaf parsley, chopped
5 slices bacon, crumbled
2 cups cooked wild rice
1 9-inch pie crust (store-bought or home-made)

Preheat oven to 450 degrees. Combine all ingredients in a large bowl. Line a 9-inch pie plate with an unbaked pastry crust. Pour in combined ingredients and bake for 10 minutes. Reduce heat to 350 degrees and bake for 30 more minutes.

WILD MUSHROOMS IN BUTTER

Wild mushrooms take to many preparations—cooked in a scramble with farm-fresh eggs, made into a cream sauce and served over pasta, or as part of a thick game stew. In any of these dishes, they add a rich and earthy flavor. But ask mushroom aficionados for their favorite recipe and "just sautéed in butter" often tops the list. Salt, pepper, lemon juice, and parsley help enhance the flavor. Use only mushrooms that you can positively identify as edible. Find guidelines for harvesting morel, oyster, sulfur shelf, and puffball mushrooms in the "Wild Mushroom Primer" in this chapter.

> 1 "find" of wild mushrooms—usually anywhere from ½ to 1 pound
> 3 tablespoons butter
> Salt and pepper to taste
> Lemon juice to taste
> ¼ cup flat leaf parsley, chopped

Begin by cleaning mushrooms. Cut morels in half lengthwise and soak in salt water; wipe clean other species with a damp cloth or paper towel. Melt butter in skillet; sauté mushrooms in butter for 5 minutes or more. Add salt, pepper, lemon juice, and parsley. Serve with crusty French bread and a chilled dry white wine such as pinot grigio or sauvignon blanc.

A Wild Mushroom Primer

Mention wild mushrooms to most Americans and you'll get a dubious look. "Poison" and "psychedelic" are the usual associations. On the other side of the pond, however, wild mushrooms are esteemed, even revered, especially in Eastern Europe. They're a central theme in literature and folklore, and are sought after with great gusto for all manner of dishes. Even children of 8 or 10 might well carry their own mushroom baskets into the woods on family outings. My aim here is not to say something profound about New World versus Old World culture, but to shed some light on an opportunity that's often overlooked by foragers—hunting for edible mushrooms in the Upper Midwest.

Should you charge right into the woods and start picking? Not without knowing some basics. There are mushrooms out there that can harm or even kill you. Fortunately, it's easy to steer clear of these poisonous mushrooms while focusing on safe species. This is done by following two rules. First, know what's bad and don't eat it. For beginners, that means ruling out all members of the Amanita family. Find them in your guidebook—always bring it with you into the woods—and simply avoid them. Yes, there are some edible species within this family, but you should leave those for experts. The second rule is to eat only those mushrooms that you can positively identify. This means making sure picked mushrooms match up with the guidebook picture and have all the characteristics specified here. If in doubt, don't pick it.

Among the vast universe of mushrooms that grow wild in the Upper Midwest, there are a number of distinctive, easy-to-identify, and delicious mushrooms. Chief among these are the morel, oyster, puffball, and sulfur shelf. These are the species we will focus on here. What's more, if one follows the directions given here and cross-references them with a photo in a guidebook, these four species can't be confused with harmful or poisonous mushrooms. So follow the description given below, get yourself a quality mushroom field guide (such as Peterson or Audubon), a small knife for cutting mushrooms free from the dirt or host log, and a mesh bag or wicker basket for holding your finds. You're now ready to head into the woods to find some great food for free. If your efforts in the woods draw a blank, you may be able to purchase wild mushrooms. Farmers' markets and natural food stores—as well as some mainstream groceries—have begun to stock a wider variety of mushrooms.

Morel mushrooms: Often hailed as the King of Mushrooms, morels are delicious indeed—and easy to identify. Known as "sponge mushrooms" in some areas, morels have a crinkly, pitted cap and a smooth stem. They're typically between 2 and 6 inches high and can be tan, gray, or brown in color. They're among the first mushrooms to emerge in spring and tend to start "popping" when the lilacs blossom, when oak leaves are the size of a squirrel's ear, when mayapples start sprouting leaves, and when trillium plants start to flower. Depending on location, they may emerge anywhere from mid-April to early June. Morel season usually lasts a few weeks to a month. The most reliable way to find morels is to know where they have sprouted in the past, and then to return to those locations. Failing that, find newly dead elm trees and search along their root lines during these times; morel mushrooms and dead elm trees have a symbiotic relationship. Abandoned apple orchards are also productive morel areas. You'll also want to scour the uplands and flood plains along major rivers—for example, Michigan's Manistee, the Mississippi, Wisconsin, Upper Iowa, Minnesota, and Red rivers—and even those of smaller rivers and streams. There's residual moisture in these areas, even in dry years, that promotes mushroom growth.

Morel mushrooms emerge first on south-facing hillsides, then move to shadier areas as the soil warms up. Cut all morel mushrooms in half lengthwise—the mushroom should be hollow inside. If there is any matter at all inside it, discard the mushroom. These may be false morels, which are not edible. If you don't find any on your own, try farmers' markets or natural food stores in areas known to produce morels. Morels take to nearly any mushroom preparation—sautéed with butter, cooked with eggs, as an enhancement to soups and stews, and as an accompaniment to grilled meat.

Oyster mushrooms: Oyster mushrooms are a favorite among mushroom hunters because they're easy to identify, have a long growing season (from summer to early winter), and are very versatile in the kitchen. While they grow in woodlands of all types, I've had the best luck finding them in moist bottomland habitats—along streams, rivers, and lakes. Dead deciduous trees play host to oyster mushrooms—willows, elms, maples, oaks, hackberries—and oysters grow, bracket-fashion, from dead and decaying logs of these species. Their average size varies, from as small as a thumb to as large as a dinner plate, but most are in the 2- to 6-inch range. Oyster mushrooms get their name from their fan-shaped cap, which resembles an oyster shell, and has pronounced gills on the underside. Their color may be gray, yellowish, or white. Oyster mushrooms may be sautéed, pickled, added to stews, or cooked with eggs. They're mild and flavorful, and pair very well with white-meat game such as pheasant, rabbit, or grouse. Harvest only young, soft mushrooms.

Sulfur shelf: While it grows in brackets from a deciduous host log like the oyster mushroom, the sulfur shelf is different from the oyster in other ways—its bright color, absence of gills, and the irregular shape of its cap. Because its color stands out, the sulfur shelf is an easy mushroom to spot in the woods. The top side of the cap is orange with a yellow rim. The texture is soft, almost like buffed leather. Depending on age and size and location, individual "shelves" may be anywhere from the size of a saucer to that of a pizza pan. Harvest young, bright-colored specimens and take only what you'll use. You can find sulfur shelf growing in the woods any time from spring until fall, especially after a heavy rain. I've even seen them in the woods as late as gun deer season in November. Many folks think sulfur shelf tastes like chicken, and I don't disagree. I like it simmered in a cream sauce, where the texture becomes something like tender chicken. As with most mushrooms, it pairs well with eggs. It can also be sautéed, along with a few shallots, in butter.

Puffballs: Everyone has seen a puffball. This big, white mushroom—often the size of a kickball or soccer ball—is easy to spot. Chances are, as a youngster, you've even gone up to one and given it a kick. But don't let that be your prevailing attitude toward puffballs. They're worth your time in the kitchen. Collect fresh, young specimens. The flesh should be firm, solid, and white—with no decay or emerging mushroom outline. Gather puffballs that are fist-size or larger. Avoid puffballs that are growing on golf courses or treated lawns, as these may contain chemicals. Once you've identified and harvested your puffball(s), refrigerate them and use within two days, as they don't keep well. They're excellent, breaded and fried, as fritters. You can fancy it up by adding herbs and seasoning to the breading, or adding onion or garlic to the frying pan.

Morel Mushroom Scramble

Scrambled eggs that have absorbed the juices of sautéed morel mushrooms are a real treat. If you don't have your own laying hens, track down fresh local eggs. Their deep color and flavor do the mushrooms justice.

4 tablespoons butter
¼ pound or more morel mushrooms, cut in half lengthwise
   (you can substitute oyster or sulfur shelf)
Salt and pepper to taste
6 farm fresh eggs, well beaten, with dollop of cream or whole milk added

Soak morels in cold salt water and then drain well. Melt butter in a large skillet and sauté mushrooms for 5 minutes. Salt and pepper to taste. Add eggs and cook lightly, turning often, until set but still soft. Serve with fresh fruit and toast for a hearty breakfast or light dinner.

Puffball Fritters

This recipe is for large puffball mushrooms that can be sliced as you would a round bread loaf. Avoid using puffballs found growing on treated lawns or golf courses, as they may contain harmful chemicals. Make sure the flesh of the puffball is solid and pure white. This is an excellent breakfast or brunch dish, served along with crisp bacon and fried eggs. Think of the puffball slices as your "toast." For best browning, make sure the butter and oil in the pan are hot but not smoking and about a ¼-inch deep. To serve puffballs as a dinner appetizer, add thyme to the batter and sauté a crushed clove of garlic or a few shallots in the pan at the last minute.

1 large puffball mushroom, cut into 1-inch-thick slices
Salt and pepper to taste
Dried chives or Penzey's Fox Point Seasoning to taste (optional)
Flour for dusting
1 egg, beaten
1 cup breadcrumbs
2 tablespoons oil
2 tablespoons butter

Wipe dry the puffball slices and season with salt, pepper, and optional seasoning; sprinkle with flour, dip in egg (letting excess egg drip off), and then dredge in bread crumbs. Heat skillet on stovetop; add oil and butter to a depth of ¼ inch and heat until hot but not smoking. Fry slices on both sides until golden-brown; keep slices on a platter in warm oven until all are ready to serve.

WILD MUSHROOM PIEROGI

There's a lot to say about pierogi, or *pirozhki*, to use the Russian spelling. They can be sweet or savory—an appetizer, a main course, or dessert. Some believe simply boiling is best, while others "finish" them by crisping in a skillet of hot butter. Among savory fillings, meat, mushrooms, cabbage, sauerkraut, and potatoes are common. Fruits—both fresh and jam—as well as a sweet farmers cheese lead the way among sweet fillings.

If you're not up for fussy pressing and folding, head out to the deli or supermarket. But if you're in the right mood—we make them on Christmas Eve—or have kitchen help, pierogi-making is fun. And the product is so satisfying! I'll pass on some tips after years of doing this. First, the dough really needs to be worked before you begin to roll it out; 20 minutes of kneading is about right. Second, a pasta-making machine helps for the final dough rolling. Also, don't overstuff them! Like making tacos, it's tempting to get as much in there as possible. But the result is usually a kitchen disaster—with filling oozing all over and a big mess to clean up. Next, make sure to press out or drain all the liquid you can. And, finally, while this recipe is for wild mushrooms, be creative with your own fillings.

Dough
5 cups white flour, plus extra for kneading and cutting
1 tablespoon salt
3 tablespoons butter, melted
1 cup whole or evaporated milk, at room temperature
1 cup warm water, as needed

Filling
1 pound wild mushrooms (morels, chicken of the woods, oyster),
    cleaned and chopped
1 large onion, peeled and chopped
Salt and pepper to taste
¼ cup butter

In a large bowl, mix together the salt and flour and scoop out a hole in the middle. Pour the butter and milk into this hole. Mix the flour and liquid together with a wooden spoon. Work or knead dough, adding water a bit at a time. You may also need to add flour to get the mixture soft and workable. When the dough is no longer sticky, turn it out on a floured cutting board or counter and knead it until soft and pliable, again adding flour or water as needed. The more you work it now, the easier it will be to roll it out later. Place dough in an oiled bowl and let rest, covered, for 30 minutes. While the dough is resting, sauté the mushrooms and onions in butter until soft. Strain through a sieve or press as much liquid from them as possible. Place drained mushrooms in a bowl. Bring 4 quarts of water to a boil on the stovetop.

Have the counter clean with three separate work areas prepared: one for rolling out dough, another for cutting dough into rounds, and one for filling. Using a pasta-making machine or rolling pin, roll out a handful of dough to desired thickness. I begin on the widest setting of our pasta maker—which is 1—and work my way up to 3 or 4. When the strip of dough is ready—between ⅛ and a 1/16 of an inch thick, about 10 inches long and 3 inches wide—begin cutting rounds from it. Flouring the edge of the cutter (Mason jar band, biscuit cutter, or water glass with 3-inch-diameter mouth) helps you make clean cuts. Now, place a tablespoon of the mushroom-onion mixture in the middle of each round. Fold the dough around it so you form a half-moon shape. Press the edges together with your fingers or crimp them with a fork. Set pierogi on oiled baking sheets, making sure edges don't touch. Spray pierogi with cooking spray. Repeat until dough is gone.

Drop dumplings in boiling water. Do not crowd. Cook until just done—about 3 minutes. Place again on baking sheets and fry, if desired, before serving. Sour cream is a time-honored accompaniment. Onions may also be sautéed in the pan along with pierogis. If you plan to freeze pierogi, allow them to cool after boiling. Once cooled, they can be sprayed with cooking spray and stored in sealed ziplock bags in the freezer.

WILD MUSHROOMS IN CREAM SAUCE

This dish is a European classic and can be taken in any number of regional directions depending on your taste and inclination. The most familiar is decidedly Italian—with the heavy cream cooked down to half, thickened with parmesan cheese, and served over pasta or gnocchi. A Middle European might substitute parsley for dried thyme, add sour cream at the last minute, and serve the works over egg noodles. A French chef would undoubtedly splash some white wine in there to deglaze the pan.

> **1 pound wild mushrooms (sulfur shelf, oyster, morel, or other),**
> **cleaned and chopped**
> **4 tablespoons butter**
> **4 shallots, chopped**
> **Salt, pepper, and thyme to taste**
> **2 cups heavy cream**
> **½ cup parmesan cheese, plus more to pass at table**

Have water for pasta at a rolling boil on the stovetop. In a large skillet, melt butter and sauté mushrooms and shallots for 5 minutes or until they have given off, then absorbed, their juices. Season with salt, pepper, and thyme. Hold mushrooms on a low heat. It is now time to synchronize the pasta and mushroom-sauce cooking; you'll want them done about the same time and it takes about 15 minutes from here to complete the mushroom sauce. Add cream to mushrooms and cook on low boil until it reduces to half. Test seasoning and adjust as necessary. Add parmesan to sauce and cook, stirring, until it's absorbed. Toss mushroom sauce in a large bowl with fresh cooked pasta or gnocchi, or place sauce dollops on each diner's bed of pasta. Pass parmesan cheese. Serve with tossed green salad, dry white wine, and crusty bread.

Wild Mushroom Risotto

Risotto originated in the rice-growing Piedmont region of northern Italy. We owe a great debt of culinary gratitude to the Italian immigrants who brought this wonderful rice dish to America. In the Upper Midwest, Italian American immigrants often settled in larger cities like Detroit, Milwaukee, and Minneapolis. A sizable population also came to work in the mines of the North Country, in Michigan, Wisconsin, and Minnesota. They foraged for mushrooms in this heavily forested area, as they'd done at home, and added them to dishes like risotto and pasta sauces. When making risotto, add broth a half-cup at a time, and then add more as this is absorbed. This process helps develop the creamy texture that makes risotto unique and delicious. Imported arborio rice can be found in Italian markets and larger grocery stores.

2 tablespoons butter, plus more as needed
2 tablespoons olive oil
1 pound wild mushrooms (oyster, morel, sulfur shelf, or a mixture of these), wiped clean and sliced
1 large onion, sliced
2 garlic cloves, minced
1 cup arborio or long-grain rice
Salt, pepper, and thyme to taste
1 quart beef, chicken, or vegetable stock
Parmesan cheese to taste
¼ cup heavy cream

In a large, wide-bottom pan or casserole, gently sauté onion and garlic in butter and oil. Add mushrooms and cook until they release their liquid. If pan is dry, add more butter. Add rice and cook until the individual grains are shiny and glazed. Season with salt, pepper, and thyme. Now, add broth a half-cup at a time and cook until liquid is absorbed. Continue this process until rice is tender. Correct seasoning. Turn off heat. Stir in parmesan cheese and cream. Allow risotto to rest for 15 minutes and serve. A dry white wine, such as pinot grigio, is a good accompaniment.

Cooking the Wild Asparagus

It seems impossible to mention wild asparagus without shouting out to Euell Gibbons, author of *Stalking the Wild Asparagus*, who's surely foraging the fertile pastures of the Great Beyond as we speak. There are a number of reasons for the book's success, including timing—it was published in 1962, just as the Back to Nature movement was getting started. The book is also encyclopedic, cataloging his foraging in all parts of the United States. Another reason for its success, I think, is its title and what that evokes: even the most casual forager has a vivid picture of wild asparagus growing along some country byway and, picturing this, is magically transported to a happier and simpler time.

Wild asparagus is delicious when picked young. It tastes of green springtime and is chock-full of B vitamins. It first starts to emerge in the southern part of Upper Midwest around the first weekend of May—the start of gamefish season in southern Wisconsin and often the beginning of morel mushrooms. Needless to say, asparagus time is a happy one for me. On a practical note, foragers need to have permission to enter private lands.

1 pound fresh asparagus, washed
Salt and pepper to taste
Olive oil to taste
Lemon juice to taste
1 garlic clove, crushed

Have a large pan of water at a rolling boil on the stovetop. Snap off tough ends of asparagus stalk (if any). Drop spears into water and cook until bright green—from 2 to 10 minutes, depending on stalk thickness. Remove, drain, and cool. Place asparagus in a casserole dish, season well with salt and pepper, then dress with olive oil and lemon juice. Spread garlic around spears and chill for 1 to 4 hours. Serve as a side with fresh-caught fish. You can also skip the marinade and eat the asparagus freshly steamed, and seasoned with salt, pepper, and butter.

Dandelion Green Salad

The irony isn't lost on frugal foragers, I think, that upscale shoppers will spend $5 a bag for organic mixed greens—the bulk of which may be dandelion—while paying a lawn service to remove this *weed* from their lawns. Be that as it may, dandelion greens are great for salad. Their tartness pairs well with the bacon slices, red onion, sweet poppyseed dressing, and boiled eggs in this recipe. For those who don't eat bacon, simply omit it. Those who really like bacon flavor can wilt the greens with hot bacon fat and reduce the amount of dressing used, but otherwise follow this recipe. Only use young, spring dandelion greens from untreated lawns.

Salad
1 cup of washed dandelion greens per person
1 red onion, sliced in thin rings
1 boiled egg per person, shelled and cut into slices
1 crisp bacon slice per person, crumbled

Dressing
1 cup canola oil
½ cup white vinegar
2 tablespoons sugar
1 teaspoon salt
1 tablespoon poppyseeds

Assemble salad ingredients in a large bowl. Whisk together dressing ingredients and pour over salad. Serve as a salad course as a side with a spring fish fry or with venison hamburgers.

Wild Greens Salad

A number of wild greens can be harvested throughout spring and summer. As with any wild edible, however, foragers must be sure of what they're picking before they eat. A quality field guide—such as Audubon or Peterson—is a must. If in doubt, you can always make a trip to your county extension office. Another caution: eat wild greens only from areas that are not treated with herbicides or other harmful chemicals.

That said, wild greens are tasty and full of vitamins. Interestingly, many of them like to grow in disturbed areas around lawns and gardens, so you needn't travel far to forage them. A quick list of what Great Lakes foragers might find around their yards and gardens includes dandelion, purselane, lamb's quarter, sheep sorrel, and curly dock weed. Purselane is a yellow-flowered, thick-stemmed plant with small leaves that resemble watercress leaves; lamb's quarter often grows in garden plots, is dusty-green in color, and is also called wild spinach because it resembles spinach; sheep sorrel has arrowhead-shaped leaves and mature plants have small red-brown flowers. If you're a gardener, don't pass up the young leaves of beets and turnips. And if you're near a cool spring or stream, watercress is an option, as well. Use the leaves and stalks of young plants; discard the roots. Harvest wild greens only from areas you know to be free of herbicides and pesticides.

The following dressing, or any favorite salad dressing, will enhance these flavorful morsels. Use 1 cup of washed greens per person. Dress with the following or any other dressing of your choice.

1 cup canola oil
½ cup white vinegar
Handful of chopped dill
Chopped red onion
Salt and pepper to taste
Pinch of sugar

FISH, GAME, AND WILDFOODS VENDORS

IOWA

Many Iowa communities have farmers' markets in them or in the surrounding area; a complete listing of Iowa farmers' markets can be found at **iafarmersmarkets.org**.
Larger farmers' markets can be found in the following communities: Ames, Bettendorf, Burlington, Cedar Falls, Cedar Rapids, Des Moines, Dubuque, Fort Dodge, Iowa City, Sioux City, Waterloo.

Bur Oak Red Deer

Fertile, IA, 3446 Dogwood Avenue, 877-252-2081 **venisonsteaks.com**
Carries a variety of venison cuts and venison products.

Great Midwest Seafood Company

Davenport, IA, 5406 Sheridan Street, 563-388-4770
Specializes in saltwater seafood, but carries Mississippi River and other freshwater fish.

Mohn Fish Market

Harpers Ferry, IA, 1144 River Road, 563-586-2269
Carries Mississippi River fish such as catfish, carp, and buffalo.

Whole Foods

West Des Moines, IA, 4100 University Avenue, 515-343-2600
Wholefoods.com
Carries pheasant, quail, duck, bison, elk, rabbit; trout, salmon, whitefish, perch, walleye, catfish; variety of mushrooms.

MICHIGAN

Many Michigan communities have farmers' markets in them or in the surrounding area; a complete listing of Michigan farmers' markets can be found at **mifma.org**. Larger farmers' markets can be found in the following communities: Ann Arbor, Cadillac, Detroit, East Tawas, Farmington, Grand Rapids, Holland, Hancock, Kalamazoo, Lansing, Leland, Munising, and Traverse City.

Browns Fish Market

Paradise, MI, Highway 28, 906-492-3901
Sells Lake Superior whitefish and lake trout—fresh, smoked, or fried.

Butcher Boy Food Products

Warren, MI, 13869 Herbert, 586-779-060 **butcherboyfoodproducts.com**
Producers of Michigan-raised bison; purveyor of wide variety of other game including venison, elk, partridge, quail, pheasant, goose, duck, rabbit, and turtle.

Gustafson's Fish Market

Brevort, MI, Highway 2, 906-292-5424
Sells Lake Superior whitefish and lake trout—fresh, smoked, or fried.

Michigan Venison Company

Traverse City, MI, PO Box 4153, 231-409-4507
Producers of venison raised on Michigan farms; for sale at farmers' markets and via telephone.

Monahan's Seafood Market

Ann Arbor, MI, 407 Fifth Street, 734-662-5118 **monahansseafood.com**
Full selection of Great Lake and other freshwater fish, located in Kerrytown Shops.

Peterson's Fish Market
Hancock, MI, 49813 US Highway 41,
906-482-2343 **exploringthenorth.com**
Sells Lake Superior fish—fresh, smoked, fried,
and caviar.

Sparrow Meat Market
Ann Arbor, MI, 407 Fifth Street,
734-761-8175 **sparrowmeat. getweb.com**
Full selection of game meats (venison, boar,
buffalo, rabbit, pheasant, quail, duck), located
in Kerrytown Shops.

Whole Foods
Ann Arbor, MI, 3135 Washnetaw Avenue,
734-975-4500
Cranbrook, MI, 900 West Eisenhower
Parkway, 734-997-7500
West Bloomfield, MI, 3135 Washnetaw
Avenue, 248-538-4600 **Wholefoods.com**
Carries pheasant, quail, duck, bison, elk, rab-
bit; trout, salmon, whitefish, perch, walleye,
catfish; variety of mushrooms.

MINNESOTA
Many Minnesota communities have farmers'
markets in them or in the surrounding area;
a complete listing of Minnesota farmers' markets can be found at **mfma.org**. Larger farmers' markets can be found in the following
communities: Baudette, Bemidji, Duluth,
Ely, Grand Rapids, Mankato, Minneapolis /
St. Paul, Red Wing, Rochester, and Thief
River Falls.

Dockside Fish Market
Grand Marais MN, 418 Minnesota Street,
218-387-2906
Specializing in Lake Superior fish—
fresh, smoked, and fried.

Gourmet Wild Game
Minneapolis, MN, 1433 Fifth Street NE,
877-ELK-MEAT **gourmetwildgame.com**
Supplier of various game meats including
venison, elk, bison, rabbit, partridge, pheasant,
quail, squab.

People's Food Co-op
Rochester, MN, 1001 Sixth Street NW,
507-289-9061 **peoplesfoodcoop.com**
Good selection of game meats and some
freshwater fish.

Russ Kendall's Smoke House
Knife River, MN, 149 Scenic Drive,
218-834-5995
Specializing in Lake Superior fish—fresh,
smoked, caviar.

Spirit Lake Nature Products
Sawyer, MN, 1032 Spirit Lake Road,
216-644-0912
Specializing in traditionally harvested wild
rice and goods produced by the Spirit Lake
band of Ojibwe.

Whole Foods
Edina, MN, 7401 France Avenue South,
952-830-3500
Maple Grove, MN, 12201 Elm Creek Boulevard N, 763-416-7300
Minneapolis, MN, 3060 Excelsior Boulevard,
612-927-8141
Minneapolis, MN, 222 Hennepin Avenue,
612-313-7101
Minnetonka, MN, 1001 Plymouth Road,
952-797-5600
St. Paul, MN, 30 South Fairview Avenue,
651-690-0197 **Wholefoods.com**
Carries pheasant, quail, duck, bison, elk, rabbit; trout, salmon, whitefish, perch, walleye,
catfish; variety of mushrooms.

WISCONSIN

Many Wisconsin communities have farmers' markets in them or in the surrounding area; a complete listing of Wisconsin farmers' markets can be found at **wifarmersmarkets.org**. Larger farmers' markets can be found in the following communities: Appleton, Bayfield, Eau Claire, Fort Atkinson, Fond du Lac, Green Bay, La Crosse, Milwaukee, Madison, Oshkosh, Phillips, Stevens Point, Sturgeon Bay, Superior, and Wausau.

Bearcat's Fish House
Algoma, WI, Highway 42,
920-487-2372
Extensive supply of Great Lakes, freshwater, and saltwater fish.

Bodin's Fisheries
Bayfield, WI, Wilson Street,
715-779-3301
Lake Superior commercial fishery selling fresh and smoked whitefish and lake trout, also whitefish caviar; will ship within Midwest.

Charlie's Smokehouse
Ellison Bay, WI, 13731 Highway 42,
920-854-2972 **charliessmokehouse.com**
Fresh and smoked whitefish, trout, and salmon; ships within U.S.

Great Lakes Gold / Dan's Fish
Sturgeon Bay, WI, 152 Jib Street,
920-743-4354 **greatlakesgold.us**
Full selection of Great Lakes and other freshwater fish; ships nationally and internationally.

MacFarlane Pheasant Farm
Janesville, WI, 2821 Highway 51,
800-345-8348 **pheasantfordinner.com**
Largest supplier of pheasants in U.S.; also carries other game meats including venison, elk, quail, and rabbit.

People's Food Co-op
La Crosse, WI, 315 South Fifth Avenue,
608-784-5798 **peoplesfoodcoop.com**
Good selection of game meats and some freshwater fish.

Rupena's Market
West Allis, WI, 7641 West Beloit Road,
414-778-2012 **rupenas.com**
Established Milwaukee butcher shop specializing in European delicacies; also carries game meats and can special order.

Schwartz's Fish Market
Sheboygan, WI, 818 Riverfront Drive,
920-452-0576
Good selection of Great Lakes and other freshwater fish.

Three Eagles Gift Shop
Ashland, WI, 66096 US Highway 2,
715-682-8844. Specializing in traditionally harvested wild rice and other goods from the Bad River band of Ojibwe.

Whole Foods
Madison, WI, 3313 University Avenue,
608-233-9566
Milwaukee, WI, 2305 N. Prospect Avenue,
414-223-1500 **Wholefoods.com**
Carries pheasant, quail, duck, bison, elk, rabbit; trout, salmon, whitefish, perch, walleye, catfish; variety of mushrooms.

Williamson Street Co-op
Madison, WI, 1221 Williamson Street,
608-251-6776
Middleton, WI, 6825 University Avenue,
608-284-7800 **willystreet.coop**
Good selection of Lake Superior and other freshwater fish.

INDEX

asparagus, wild: harvesting, 129-30; recipe, 158

bear, black: cleaning, 3, 4, 5; recipes, 28-30
beaver: cleaning, 33, 34; recipe, 47
berries: blintzes with, 137; buttermilk pancakes with, 138; cobbler, 142; harvesting, 130-32; jam and syrup, 139-40
black bear. *See* bear, black
blackberries: harvesting, 130-32; recipes, 137-39, 142
blackcaps. *See* black raspberries
black duck: hunting/harvesting, 66-68; recipes, 69-80
black raspberries: harvesting, 130-31; recipes, 137-39, 141, 142
black walnuts. *See* walnuts, black
blini, whitefish caviar with, 123
blueberries: harvesting, 132, 137-39, 142
bluebill (duck): hunting/harvesting, 66-68; recipes, 55, 74, 76
bluegill: harvesting, 97; recipes, 106, 108, 110
bobwhite quail. *See* quail
bufflehead: hunting/harvesting, 66-68; recipes, 55, 74, 76
bullhead: harvesting, 97; recipes, 76, 108
burgers, venison, 7
butchering: deer and other big game, 3-5

Cajun/Creole recipes, 41, 76, 78
Canada goose: hunting/harvesting, 66-68; recipes, 72, 80, 81, 85-89
canvasback (duck): hunting/harvesting, 66-68; recipes, 69-80
catfish: harvesting, 97; recipes, 76, 108
caviar, whitefish, 123, 124, 125
cherries: harvesting, 132; recipes, 55, 142, 154
chicken-of-the-woods mushroom: harvesting, 134-36, 148-51; recipes, 147, 154-57
chili, venison, 9

chowder, 121
Chronic Wasting Disease (CWD), 4
cobbler, fruit, 142
commercial fishing in Upper Midwest, 108
coot, 90
crappie: harvesting, 97; recipes, 106, 108, 110
crawfish, 120
Crock-Pot, recipes using, 18, 88, 101
currants, recipes using, 21, 58, 63, 83, 145, 154

dandelion greens, recipes using, 158, 159
deer: butchering and field dressing, 3-4; cooking, 4-5; hunting, 1-3; obtaining farm-raised meat, 58-59, 161-63; recipes, 6-14, 17-24
diving ducks: hunting/harvesting, 66-68; recipes, 55, 74, 76
dove: hunting/harvesting, 49-50; recipes, 60, 62
ducks: breasting, 67, 68; cleaning, 67, 68; diving vs. puddle, 66, 67; hunting, 64, 65; plucking, 67, 68; recipes, 69-81, 85; species, 66, 67

Eastern European-influenced recipes, 18, 19, 20, 22, 30, 55, 72, 89, 115, 122, 123, 125, 154
egg-based recipes, 146, 152

fish: cleaning, 96-97; freezing, 97; recipes, 98-112, 115-17, 121-23, 125-26; species, 91
fishing, 92-96
fruit: in game recipes, 17, 45, 54, 55, 63, 74, 87; gathering wild, 130-32, 136; in sweets/desserts, 137-41

gadwall: hunting/harvesting, 66-68; recipes, 69-80
goldeneye: hunting/harvesting, 66-68; recipes, 55, 74, 76
goose: hunting/harvesting, 64, 67; recipes, 80, 81, 85-90
Great Lakes: duck hunting, 64, 66; fishing, 91, 92, 95-96

grouse, ruffed: hunting/harvesting, 49-51; recipes, 35, 55, 61

grouse, sharptail: hunting/harvesting, 49–51; recipes, 55, 61

hare, snowshoe: hunting/harvesting, 34; recipes, 43, 46

hazelnuts, 134

hickory nuts: harvesting, 133-34; recipes, 142, 144

jam, berry, 139

lake trout: fishing, 91, 103; recipes, 99, 121

mallard: hunting/harvesting, 66-68; recipes, 69-80

Mississippi River: duck hunting, 65, 75; fishing, 91, 93, 95, 96, 103-5, 112, 118

morel mushrooms: harvesting, 128-29, 148, 150; recipes, 72, 152, 154, 157, 158

mushrooms: harvesting, 128-29, 134-36, 148-51; recipes, 25, 26, 40, 57, 71, 72, 147, 152-57

northern pike: harvesting, 91, 92, 93, 94, 96; recipes, 115, 121, 122, 126

nuts: harvesting, 132-34; recipes, 142, 133

O'Brien, Cecilia, recipe from, 132, 140

O'Brien, Dan, recipes from, 55, 60, 61

oyster mushrooms: harvesting, 134-35, 148, 150; recipes, 57, 71, 147, 152, 155, 157, 158

panfish: harvesting, 92, 95; recipes, 109, 115, 122

partridge. See grouse, ruffed

perch, yellow: buying commercially raised, 161-63; harvesting, 92, 95; recipes, 109, 115, 122

pheasant, ringneck: buying commercially raised, 58-59, 161-63; hunting/harvesting, 48-52; recipes, 52-57, 63

pickled fish, 96; recipe, 115

pig, wild: harvesting, 5; recipes, 28, 31

pintail (duck): hunting/harvesting, 66-68; recipes, 69-80

potpie recipes, 13, 14, 40, 86

puffball mushrooms: harvesting, 134-35, 148, 151; recipe, 153

quail: buying commercially raised, 58-59, 161-63; hunting/harvesting, 49-52; recipes, 60, 62

rabbit: buying commercially raised, 58-59, 161-63; hunting/harvesting, 32-34; recipes, 40-45, 76

raccoon, 34

redhead duck: hunting/harvesting, 66-68; recipes, 69-80

redhorse (fish): harvesting, 96; recipe, 115

ringneck duck: hunting/harvesting, 66-68; recipes, 69-80

ringneck pheasant. See pheasant, ringneck

ruffed grouse. See grouse, ruffed

Russian-influenced recipes, 22, 25, 30, 72, 122, 123, 125, 137, 153

salmon: Great Lakes fishing, 91, 92, 103-4; recipes, 99, 101

sauerkraut, in game recipes, 55, 89, 154

sausage: making, 21-23; recipes, 20, 22, 76, 80, 145

scaup. See bluebill

sheepshead (fish): harvesting, 96, 97; recipe, 116

sharptail grouse. See grouse, sharptail

shoveler (duck): harvesting, 66-68; recipe, 74

smelt: harvesting, 96; recipe, 107

smoker, making from barrel, 113-14

smoking/smoke cooking, 113-14; recipes, 22, 112

snapping turtle: buying commercially, 118, 161-63; recipes, 118, 119

snowshoe hare. See hare, snowshoe

snow goose: hunting/harvesting, 66-68; recipes, 72, 80, 81, 85-89

sucker (fish): harvesting, 96; recipe, 115

teal: harvesting, 66-68; recipes, 69-80

trout: cleaning, 96-97; Great Lakes fishing, 92, 95-96; inland fishing, 93-95; recipes, 98, 99, 100, 121, 122

turtle. See snapping turtle

upland game. *See* dove; grouse, ruffed; grouse, sharptail; pheasant, ringneck; wild turkey; woodcock

venison: butchering and field dressing, 3-4; cooking, 4-5; obtaining farm-raised meat, 58-59, 161-63; recipes, 6-14, 17-24

walleye: buying from commercial sources, 161-63; harvesting, 93, 95, 97; recipes, 106, 109, 11, 121, 122

walnuts, black: cooking/harvesting, 132, 134

watercress: harvesting, 128; recipe, 161

waterfowl. *See* ducks; goose

Weiss, Denny, recipes from, 9, 47, 106, 119

whitefish: buying, 103-5, 161-63; caviar, 123-25; commercial fishing on Great Lakes, 103-5; recipes, 102, 122

whitefronted goose: hunting/harvesting, 66-68; recipes, 72, 80, 81, 85-89

whitetailed deer. *See* deer; venison

wigeon (duck): harvesting, 66-68; recipes, 69-80

wild asparagus. *See* asparagus, wild

wild pig. *See* pig, wild

wild rice: harvesting, 82-84; recipes, 80, 81, 146

wild turkey: hunting/harvesting, 50-51; recipes, 60, 63

woodcock: hunting/harvesting, 49, 50; recipes, 60, 61

wood duck: harvesting, 66-68; recipes, 69-80

yellow perch. *See* perch, yellow

12/14-WS